Leader's Guide for use with

THE PILLARS OF MARRIAGE

H. Norman Wright

GL Regal Books A Division of G/L Publications
Glendale, California, U.S.A.

The foreign language publishing of all Regal books is under the direction of *Gospel Literature International* (GLINT), a missionary assistance organization founded in 1961 by Dr. Henrietta C. Mears. Each year *Gospel Literature International* provides financial and technical help for the adaptation, translation and publishing of books and Bible study materials in more than 85 languages for millions of people worldwide.

For more information you are invited to write *Gospel Literature International,* Glendale, California 91204.

Scripture quotations in this publication are from the following versions:

NASB: *New American Standard Bible.* © The Lockman Foundation 1960, 1962, 1963, 1968, 1971. Used by permission.

AMP: *The AMPLIFIED BIBLE,* Copyright © 1962, 1964 by Zondervan Publishing House. Used by permission.

TLB: *The Living Bible,* Copyright © 1971 by Tyndale House Publishers, Wheaton, Illinois. Used by permission.

Phillips: *THE NEW TESTAMENT IN MODERN ENGLISH,* Revised Edition, J.B. Phillips, Translator. © J.B. Phillips 1958, 1960, 1972. Used by permission of Macmillan Publishing Co., Inc.

RSV: *Revised Standard Version* of the Bible, copyrighted 1946 and 1952 by the Division of Christian Education of the NCCC, U.S.A., and used by permission.

NEB: *The New English Bible.* The Delegates of the Oxford University Press and the Syndics of the Cambridge University Press 1961, 1970. Reprinted by permission.

KJV: The Authorized King James Version.

Published by Regal Books Division, G/L Publications
Glendale, California 91209
Printed in U.S.A.

ISBN 0-8307-0699-2

Contents

Introduction

Marriage is a God-ordained relationship and institution. It can be a relationship in which each person develops and enhances his own life and helps his partner do the same; or it can be marked by stagnation, which leads either to a miserable coexistence or to dissolution of the marriage.

For a marriage to develop to its full potential, the partners must plan, accept, and be flexible. This series of sessions for married couples is designed to build and enrich the marriage relationship. This is not a lecture series, but one in which the couples will do most of the thinking, communicating, planning, and work. These sessions have been used in Sunday School classes, weekend retreats, extended family camps, and marriage enrichment seminars for lay couples, professional marriage educators, and ministers.

Those attending your classes will gain the most by attending with their spouses. Many of the activities are designed in such a manner that each couple will be talking and working together for 10 to 15 minutes. If you have several in your class who come without their spouses, you may ask them to discuss the material in a small group of their own.

How to Use Transparencies

The transparencies and reproduction masters in this manual are perforated for easy removal. To remove each transparency, hold the book binding in your left hand, grasp the transparency with your right hand and carefully pull it out from top to bottom. You may want to mount each transparency in a transparency frame to better protect it and make it easier to handle.

We suggest that, when you use the transparency on the overhead projector, you cover it with a piece of paper or cardboard and reveal only as much as you are teaching from at a time. This way your class stays with you as you progress through the activity.

How to Use Reproduction Masters

The reproduction masters may be photocopied or used as camera-ready copy for quick-print offset press, electronic stencils or Dittomasters. If you cut your own stencils you must include the publishers' credit line found at the bottom of each reproduction master and transparency.

Be sure to save the reproduction master for reuse.

Advance Preparation

For each session you will need:
- an overhead projector
- butcher paper or newsprint (for brainstorming sessions)
- marking pens
- paper and pencils
- chalkboard, chalk, eraser (or large sheets of paper and felt pens)
- blank transparencies
- several versions of the Bible

Session 1
- Reproduce "Marriage Evaluation Form"
- Have available "American Family Life Today" transparency

Session 2
- Have available "Things People Blame" transparency

Session 3
- Reproduce "What Is Your Opinion?"

Session 4
- Have available "Expectations and Goals in Marriage" transparency

Session 5
- Have available "Ten Commandments for Married Couples" transparency

Session 6
- Reproduce "In-Law Relationships" (2 pages); "Love Response Visualization Form" (3 pages)
- Have available "Ten Commandments for Married Couples" and "Three Types of Love" transparencies

Session 7
- Read 1 Kings 18—19 three times
- Reproduce "Holmes-Rahe Stress Test"
- Have available "Discussion Questions About Stress" and "Being 'In Christ' " transparency

Session 8
- Reproduce "Grief and Ministry"
- Have available the two "Grief" transparencies

Session 9
- Reproduce "Your Percentage of the Decision Analysis"
- Have available "Decision-Making in Marriage" transparency

Session 10
- Reproduce "Conflict" and "The Counselor's Game"

Session 11
- Reproduce "Conflict Analysis"
- Have available "Five Styles of Handling Conflict/How to Resolve Conflict" and "Conflict" transparencies
- Have available a copy of *The Living Bible*

Session 12
- Reproduce "Forgiveness Sentence Completion"
- Have available "Forgiveness—What it Is, What it Isn't" transparency

Guidelines For Leading These Sessions

1. For your own information concerning the teaching methods used in this course, read *Learning Is Change* by Martha Leypoldt (Judson Press).

2. If you have never taught a course on marriage relationships, or if the people in your group or class have never taken one, you may want to start with another course first, using this series later as an advanced study. The suggested basic course is *Communication: Key to Your Marriage*. The leader's manual and student book are published by Regal Books and should be available through your local church supplier.

3. Be sure you read this course through completely before teaching it. To teach effectively you will need to spend several hours in study for the course. In addition you will need time to prepare the materials and decide which activities to use in each session.

4. Do not attempt to bring all of the church couples into this course at once. You need a minimum of 8 to 10 couples and a maximum of 20. If many couples are interested, you may offer more than one class or have a waiting list for the next course. While this material can be taught to large groups using the same methods, the ideal is a smaller group so that you can become better acquainted with the class members and so that they may have more opportunities to ask you questions and to develop relationships within the class.

5. You will need at least 60 minutes for each session. For one session you will need at least 70 minutes. If you meet on Sunday morning you may want to start the class 15 minutes earlier than usual and use all of the time for this series. (Eliminate announcements, singing, and other "preliminaries.") It is better to present thoroughly the main ideas than to stop before changes occur in the lives of class members. Be aware of the suggested time structure for each activity, but at the same time be flexible and adaptable to the needs of your group.

6. Read the Advance Preparation section for each session very carefully, and order all materials at least one month in advance.

7. When having people work in groups, unless it is otherwise stated, encourage spouses to be in the same discussion group. Those without spouses present can discuss in a separate group if there are enough.

8. To learn more about marriage relationships, read the following books; they will enrich your teaching.

No Fault-Marriage by Marcia Lasswell and Norman Lobsenz (Ballantine Books)

Why Marriage? by Edward Ford (Argus)

Communication: Key to Your Marriage by H. Norman Wright (Regal)

Family Communication by Sven Wahlroos (Macmillan)

As an added resource, write to CME, 8000 E. Girard, Suite 601, Denver, Colorado 80231, for a sample copy of the magazine *Marriage—The Magazine of Marital Enrichment,* and for sufficient brochures for your class members.

Many churches are spending hundreds of dollars a year to bring in outside speakers to conduct marriage seminars and classes. If you have your ministerial staff or selected laymen within your church learn to conduct them, these classes will be more effective. This way the courses can be offered again and again, providing an ongoing ministry as well as follow-up. Many who take these classes can be trained to teach them to others within the church or in home Bible studies. By spending $25 to $75, your church can develop better resources and a more helpful class than by employing outside specialists to teach the series. Developing the program will take work and planning, but the results will be more extensive and longer lasting.

(Note: Some of the material in this course is original; some has been adapted from ideas of other educators and graduate students.)

Looking at Marriage

OBJECTIVES

1. To clarify and identify specific facts and beliefs concerning marriage and family life today.

2. To have participants evaluate their own marriages.

3. To identify specific steps each couple can take to strengthen their marriage in each area evaluated.

ADVANCE PREPARATION

1. Duplicate the "Marriage Evaluation Form." Make a copy for each person in your class.

2. Have available an overhead projector and "American Family Life Today," the transparency for this session.

Time: 60–65 minutes

Activity: TRIADS

Time: 15 minutes

Begin this session by welcoming those who have come. Give them a brief overview of the course. Then divide the group into triads (groups of three). Ask them to number off 1 to 3. Each triad should be made up of people who do not know each other very well. Every person in the triad will have two minutes in which to tell the other two people their response to this statement: "This is what you need to know about my marriage in order to understand me as a person." At the end of two minutes the two listeners can ask any questions they like, which the responder must answer. This exchange will take about one minute. Then another person will give a response to the topic statement for two minutes, and answer questions for one minute, until all three have responded.

After the individuals have formed their groups and you have given the instructions, ask those who are number 3 to begin sharing. At the completion of this activity ask for reactions from everyone. Ask them how they felt during the past nine minutes as they shared. Ask how many married couples spend as much time talking to each other about the things they have just shared in their groups; how many couples communicate on this level; how many people can even listen to his partner for two minutes without speaking?

Activity: LECTURE

Time: 15 minutes

Use the following material to give the class an update on facts and attitudes concerning marriage today in our country. Use the transparency for portions of this information. Be sure to share the information that is not on the transparency.

Is there a crisis in American family life today? The following facts and statements represent the deepening concern.

In the report on the American family by *Better Homes and Gardens* (1972), of the more than 340,000 respondents, 71 percent felt that "American family life is in trouble." Sixty-four percent of them said that America is a worse place to rear children than it was 10 to 15 years ago. Only 11 percent felt that most couples are well prepared for marriage, and *85 percent felt that religion has lost its influence on family life today.*[1]

The 1978 *Better Homes and Gardens* report included 302,000 respondents. Here are some of the questions and responses.

Do you feel that family life in America is in trouble?
    Yes: 76 percent   No: 22 percent
The greatest threat to family life in descending order are:
    Inattentive parents: 37 percent
    Absence of religious and spiritual foundation: 36 percent
    Materialism: 21 percent
    Financial pressure: 18 percent
    Divorce: 18 percent
If you had it to do over, would you have children?
    Yes: 91 percent   No: 9 percent
Do working parents spend enough time with their children?
    Fathers—No: 86 percent   Working mothers—No: 72 percent
What is the greatest influence on the general development of children under age 12?
    Parents: 84 percent
    Television: 48 percent

Friends: 40 percent
Teachers: 33 percent
Church: 19 percent

Is America a better or worse place to rear children than it was 10 to 15 years ago?

Better: 15 percent; Same: 26 percent; Worse: 58 percent

In your opinion, are teenagers today more qualified or less qualified to make independent value judgments than was true 10 years ago?

More qualified: 37 percent; Less qualified: 19 percent; No change: 42 percent

Which better prepares youngsters for the future—a strict home environment or a permissive one?

Strict: 73 percent; Permissive: 20 percent

Most readers touted a combination.

Are most of your expectations of happiness in marriage being fulfilled?

Yes: 85 percent; No: 15 percent

Would you consider a decline in the husband's dominance to be beneficial or harmful to family life?

Beneficial: 45 percent; Harmful: 52 percent

Seventy-six percent agree that the traditional role of wife and mother as a full-time homemaker can lead to a fulfilling life.

Do you think it's right or wrong for a couple who simply can't get along to get a divorce?

When no children are involved:
  Right: 84 percent; Wrong: 12 percent
When children are involved:
  Right: 75 percent; Wrong: 22 percent

Readers felt the main reasons why marriages fail are:

Immaturity: 61 percent
Selfishness: 51 percent
Changes in or lack of mutual interests and goals: 44 percent
Financial problems: 41 percent
Third-party entanglements: 24 percent
Personality conflicts: 22 percent
Poor sexual adjustments: 16 percent
Job pressures: 14 percent
Burden of children: 10 percent

Seventy-two percent feel that religion is losing influence on family life.[2]

Twenty-five hundred professional family life educators and marriage counselors participating in the National Alliance for Family Life Research (1973) said: "There is a definite need for strengthening family life in our nation today." Sixty-six percent of them said that "churches are *not* doing an adequate job of promoting and maintaining family life as a contemporary concept." Ninety-three percent felt that young people are *not* receiving adequate preparation for marriage from their parents.[3]

Families are disrupted in many ways today. Desertion accounts for more family breakups than most realize. We hear much about divorce, too. For example, in 1972 for every 1,000 marriages that occurred, 455 divorces also occurred. The *Los Angeles Times* reported that in Orange County, California, during the first six months of 1974 there were 6,372 marriages and 6,702 divorces.[4]

In the May 15, 1978, issue of *Newsweek* magazine, the latest statistics were given. This report, entitled "The Marriage Odds," indicated that 96 percent of all Americans will marry, and 38 percent of this group will divorce. Of the 38 percent who divorce,

79 percent will remarry and 44 percent will divorce again.[5]

Divorce is only one situation with which we are confronted in our ministries. The majority of homicides committed in our nation are acts perpetrated against other family members. FBI statistics report that police across the nation receive more calls for family conflicts than for murders, aggravated batteries, and all other serious crimes. The statistics also show that 26 percent of all police fatalities occur while investigating domestic disturbances. All of these various difficulties happen to people within our churches. The tragedy is, however, that we often fail to hear about them because of fear, concern, or guilt on the part of the church member.

The ultimate depth of pessimism is seen in the words of Nathan Ackerman concerning the family situation: "I am a psychiatrist who has devoted a lifetime to studying emotional problems of family living. I have pioneered in the field of family therapy. From where I sit, the picture of marriage and family in present-day society is a gloomy one. Family life seems to be cracking at the seams, and an effective mortar is nowhere available."[6]

There is, however, an effective mortar: the person of Jesus Christ. The presence of Christ, the ministry of the Holy Spirit, and intense effort and work dedicated to the application of Scripture can bring stability, growth, and mutual satisfaction into a marital relationship.

John Lavendar, in *Your Marriage Needs Three Love Affairs*, cites seven needs from the Bible that Christian marriage is designed to meet.

Your marriage needs *completion* (see Gen. 2:18,24). Couples who complete each other are friends. A friend is one with whom you feel comfortable, who believes in you, who shares your concerns and hurts as well as your ideas, beliefs and philosophies.

Your marriage needs *communication* (see Phil. 2:1-4). Learn 25:11). Being married gives you the opportunity to become a channel of God's healing grace. To speak a word of encouragement and support to your spouse fulfills the need for consolation.

Your marriage needs *communication* (see Phil. 2:1–4). Learn to know and understand your mate through effective communication—with Christ and each other.

Your marriage needs *coition* or sexual fulfillment (see Gen. 1:28; Prov. 5:18,19). Sexuality is our celebration of God's continuing creativity, even when it is meant as an act of joyous communion with no intention of conception.

The need for *creation* was meant to be satisfied through the marriage relationship.

Your marriage needs *correlation* (see Eph. 4:15,16). The husband and wife relationship, or the family life, should be a church in miniature so that they reflect to the non-Christian community what the Body of Christ is like.

Your marriage needs *Christianization* (see Josh. 24:15; Eph. 6:4). Living the Christian life in a family, though difficult, has a greater effect upon the world than any other form of evangelization.

Activity: INDIVIDUAL WORK

Time: 15–20 minutes

David and Vera Mace, pioneers in the field of marital enrichment, suggest a helpful test designed to help couples discover the present stage of growth of their marriage. This brief test can be scored by you, and you won't be turning it in. (**Distribute the "Marriage Evaluation" form to class members.**) It is important that you work alone on this "Marriage Evaluation" form.

Try to estimate just where *your* marriage is in the 10 areas listed on the form:

1. Common goals and values
2. Commitment to growth
3. Communication skills
4. Creative use of conflict
5. Appreciation and affection
6. Agreement on gender roles
7. Cooperation and teamwork
8. Sexual fulfillment
9. Money management
10. Decision-making

Take each area in turn and decide upon a score from 1 to 10 for each one. To decide your score, first consider where your marriage *could* be. What would it be like if you had both together made all the progress you could possibly make in the area concerned—learned all you could, worked together at it to the best of your abilities, sought all the outside help you might need? This would be the full 10 points.

Next, where is your marriage *now*—how far have you already traveled toward the fulfillment of your full potential? Give yourself a score, from 1 to 10, to represent your present level of achievement.

Remember, you are scoring your *marriage*—not just your own part in it. You should do this carefully and honestly. But be fair to yourselves and give yourselves credit for whatever you have already accomplished.

One good way to find your score is to run fairly quickly through the list and spontaneously write in scores in pencil; then go back over them all more carefully and critically and change any scores you don't feel are exactly accurate.

When you have scored yourselves in all of the areas, add up the numbers. This will give you the percentage of your estimated potential that you have already achieved. Subtract this number from 100, and you will have the percentage of your marital potential that you still have to appropriate.[7]

Activity: GROUP DISCUSSION

Time: 15 minutes

Divide the class into groups of three couples each. Ask them to suggest three positive steps a couple could take for each of the 10 items listed to improve their marriage in these areas. Each group should appoint a recorder to make a list of the group's suggestions. After 8 to 10 minutes ask the various groups to share their steps.

CONCLUSION

As you conclude, also ask husbands and wives to compare with each other their percentage scores of achieved potential indicated on their "Marriage Evaluation" forms. Then instruct them as follows:

If your scores are very close, this means that you are both in fairly complete agreement about where your marriage is. If there is a significant difference in your percentages, your standards of evaluation are not the same, and it would be a good idea to find out why. Low scores may mean poor performances, but they may also mean high expectations. You need to examine differing views, either of your performance or of your expectations, to see what lies behind them.

Now together go over your individual scores for each of the 10 areas. Again you may find some in close agreement. Wide differences need to be looked at together, and you may gain some important insights by discussing them. If in some areas you both have low scores, you can quickly agree that these are areas on which you have some work to do. Don't take a pessimistic view of low scores; they mean you have good things coming to you that you haven't yet claimed.

Most couples find taking this test a very revealing and helpful experience. Most tell us that this is the first time they have ever really taken an honest look at where they are in their relationship. Some couples who thought they had excellent relationships are quite surprised. One couple said: "We have been shaken out of our complacency. Now we've got to get to work."[8]

Complete chapter 1 in the text before the next session.

Conclude your session with prayer.

Notes

1. "Report on the American Family," *Better Homes and Gardens*, 1972.
2. "Report on the American Family," *Better Homes and Gardens*, 1978.
3. *National Alliance for Family Life Newsletter*, Spring, 1973. Huntington Beach, CA.
4. *Los Angeles Times*, November, 1974.
5. "The Marriage Odds," *Newsweek*, May 15, 1978, p. 67.
6. Nathan Ackerman, in Harold H. Hart, ed., *Marriage: For and Against* (New York: Hart Publishing Company, Inc., 1971), p. 12.
7. David and Vera Mace, *How to Have a Happy Marriage* (Nashville: Abingdon Press, 1977), pp. 53,54. Copyright 1977, used by permission.
8. Mace, pp. 54,55. Copyright 1977, used by permission.

Excuses for Marital Difficulties

OBJECTIVES

1. To identify typical excuses people use to hinder marital growth.

2. To clarify and identify personal excuses participants use in their marriages.

3. To identify and apply specific biblical teaching concerning excuses and defensiveness in marriage.

ADVANCE PREPARATION

Have available an overhead projector and the transparency for this session, "Things People Blame."

Time: 60 minutes

Activity: LECTURE

Time: 10 minutes

One of the tendencies of human nature is to project blame onto others for difficulties, problems, or circumstances. When people have difficulty in marriage they seem to resort to two procedures: (1) they defend themselves; and (2) they try to discover why the other person does what he does. They think they'll be happy when they know *why* the other person acts as he does. However, knowing why a person does something doesn't necessarily solve the problem.

Finding out *why* is not always important, nor is it always possible. What is important is spending time determining what is going on in a relationship and making plans for solving the difficulties or making the necessary changes. Reasons may be important at times, but too often they are used as excuses!

Let's look at some typical excuses that people use when they consider why their marriage isn't what they want it to be.

(Use the transparency and read through this list with the class. Cover the transparency with a white piece of paper and reveal each statement one at a time.)

Some people blame their health

I've had this cold for three months now.

I have migraine headaches and...

I'm just tired all the time.

My metabolism is just different than yours.

Some people blame their feelings

My nerves are so shaky, and you don't help them at all.

I've been depressed.

The kids make me so upset.

Some people blame their nature

I'm just this way, that's all. I always have been.

I can't change.

I'm a phlegmatic—you know what they're like.

Some people blame others

Her mother is always...

His friends are really...

It's the darn kids. They just never go to sleep at the right time.

My boss just gets to me. And then...

Some people blame the past

She has always been that way.

Nobody has ever liked me and they never will.

My other marriage was lousy too.

My mother always used to put me down.

Some people blame their partners

He makes me so upset I could scream.

If only she'd shut up and listen to me.

He's an animal. All he thinks about is food, TV, and sex, and not in that order either!

If she'd ever clean the house I'd faint.

Some people blame "why"

Why don't we communicate?

If only I could understand why he does...

But why can't he stay home on Saturday nights?

Activity: PERSONAL EVALUATION

Time: 5 minutes

Leave the transparency on the projector and ask everyone to write down which of these they heard in their own homes as they were growing up. Then ask them to write down which ones they use. Be sure they understand they are not writing down what their partner says but the excuses they themselves use.

Activity: GROUP DISCUSSION

Time: 10 minutes

Ask the class to meet in groups of three (not with their spouses) and to list other excuses they have heard and excuses Christians might be guilty of using. After several minutes, ask for several of their responses.

Activity: CLASS DISCUSSION

Time: 5–10 minutes

Ask each person to write down why people might be defensive and use excuses. Then in a general, open discussion, ask class members to share some of these reasons. Some class members may begin to get some insight into their own behavior. Remind them that it isn't always important for us to know why the other person is doing what he is doing; but if the person himself can begin to think of why he is using excuses, it may help him.

Activity: BIBLE STUDY

Time: 15 minutes

Ask the members to form groups of three or four and to search through the book of Proverbs, chapters 10 through 30, to see if they can find guidelines that would apply to the matter of excuses. They are looking for instructions to those who make excuses and for principles that help those who must deal with a person who makes excuses. After the groups have had time to search, ask for several responses from the entire group.

Activity: LECTURE

Time: 10 minutes

Read the following Scriptures to the class from the version indicated. (They are reprinted in chapter 2 of the text for this course.) These verses apply to those who make excuses:

The Living Bible: Proverbs 13:18; 25:11; 28:13,23
The Amplified Bible: Proverbs 10:17; 15:1,32; 17:10; 19:11; 27:5.

Then share these passages which might help us in responding to a person who relies upon excuses:

The Amplified Bible: Ephesians 4:15,25; Proverbs 12:18; 18:13.

A person who makes excuses may feel threatened or insecure. He may have a poor self-image. He may be fearful that his admission may be used against him time and time again and that he'll never hear the last of it.

We can help such a person by not accusing or attacking him when we ask a question. When a person admits a mistake or doing something wrong, we can thank the person and then ask if there is anything that we can do to help the situation. The less pressure we put upon the person, the better chance there is for a positive response.

There are just two items that we should consider as we close. The first is, when we can stop making excuses about what we can't do in our marriage and why we can't do it, then we can put forth our effort on building the marriage.

Second, what does making excuses accomplish? Do our excuses solve the problem, create more problems, or just postpone the problems? What would happen if we would begin to admit our mistakes? Perhaps others would learn to take pressure off us. If we have children who make excuses and defend themselves, could it be that they learned this pattern from us? Could they be insecure? What can we do to help them?

Ask individuals to write down an excuse they use and would be willing to replace with an honest response.

CONCLUSION

Remind the participants to read and complete chapter 2 in the text. Ask them to bring their books with them each session.

Close with prayer.

The Most Important Elements of Marriage

OBJECTIVES

1. To identify beliefs and attitudes toward factors that influence a marriage relationship.
2. To begin to identify the characteristics that will enhance a marriage relationship.

ADVANCE PREPARATION

1. Duplicate the agree-disagree form for this session, "What Is Your Opinion?"
Time: 60 minutes

Activity: AGREE-DISAGREE

Time: 40–45 minutes

Distribute the "What Is Your Opinion" agree-disagree sheet together with pencils. Then give the following instructions:

Each of you has been given an agree-disagree sheet. On the sheet you will find several statements concerning the specifics of the marriage relationship. I would like each of you (individually and without talking with anyone else) to read each statement and decide whether you agree or disagree with each statement as it is presented there. Read it carefully and decide what you think. If you agree, place a check mark in the appropriate blank marked "agree." If you disagree, place a check in the blank marked "disagree." You will be given enough time to answer the statements. Please work individually and as quickly as possible.

Give the class enough time to complete their work. When everyone has finished, thank them for completing the sheet. Then ask all those who agreed with statement number one to raise their hands. Then ask how many of them disagreed with statement number one. Proceed to statement number two and ask how many agreed and how many disagreed. Do this for each of the agree-disagree statements without stopping to discuss any of the statements. When you finish, divide the class into groups of eight with equal number of men and women in each group if possible.

Let the groups discuss the agree-disagree statements. The people should share not only what they answered on the agree-disagree section, but why. What was the basis or reason for their answers? They do not have to discuss all of the statements but may discuss those they are most interested in or those about which the class had the most differences of opinion. Be sure to let them know they can share any of their opinions.

As the teacher-leader you should circulate from group to group and listen to the interaction of your class members. Allow sufficient time for the groups to really get involved in these statements.

An alternative to this style of discussion with an agree-disagree form is to ask those who agree to go and stand at one side of the room and those who disagree to go and stand on the other side of the room. Then each side tells why they answered the way they did. You will find that this procedure will generate a lively discussion. After sufficient time use the same procedure for the next question.

Activity: COUPLE BRAINSTORMING OR INDIVIDUAL WORK

Time: 10 minutes

On the basis of your answers to the agree-disagree form, couples will get together and make a list of what you believe are the 10 most important elements of a marriage relationship. If you are here without your spouse, form your own list.
(Give the class enough time to complete their work. Then ask several to share their lists.)

CONCLUSION

Remind the couples to complete chapter 3. Also ask them to take the agree-disagree sheet and search through the Bible to discover specific passages which they feel would answer the statements.

Conclude with prayer.

Expectations and Goals in Marriage

OBJECTIVES

1. To identify reasons men and women marry.

2. To identify what couples are receiving from their marriage.

3. To identify and evaluate past and present marital expectations.

4. To identify and evaluate goals Christian couples should have for their marriage.

ADVANCE PREPARATION

1. Have paper and pencils available.

2. Have the overhead projector and the transparency "Expectations and Goals in Marriage" available.

Time: 60–70 minutes

Activity: Brainstorming

Time: 10 minutes

After everyone has arrived, divide the class into groups of four. Men should be with men and women with women. Tell them that they will now function as brainstorming groups, which means that they will list as many ideas as possible in response to the questions that you will give to them. They are not to discuss the answers or evaluate them, but simply list them. They will have four minutes for this activity. The questions are: "For what reasons do men marry?" "For what reasons do women marry?" (Use the transparency and show these questions on the screen.) Have class members spend two minutes on each of the questions in their groups, and be sure that one person in each group writes the answers. After the four-minute brainstorming activity is completed, ask several of the groups to give their reasons for marriage. You will find that the reporting will elicit some reaction and humor.

Activity: INDIVIDUAL WORK

Time: 6–8 minutes

Ask everyone to take pencil and paper and individually write their answers to this question: "What are you getting out of marriage that you wouldn't have if you had remained single?" Give them three minutes to answer the question. Then ask them to answer this question: "What do you think your spouse is getting out of marriage that he wouldn't have if he had remained single?" Show both of these questions on the screen. When they have answered the questions, ask the groups to keep their answers; they will use the answers later. Their homework assignment will be to share their answers to these two questions with their spouse.

Activity: GROUP DISCUSSION

Time: 6–8 minutes

Have the class divide into groups of four, and for six to eight minutes discuss the question, "What should a person get out of marriage that he wouldn't get by remaining single?" Show the question on the screen. At the end of this time, ask some of the groups to share some of their answers with the whole class.

Emphasize that there are many people today who have no real answer to this question, for they are not getting very much out of their marriages. In order to get something from marriage, a couple must be willing to put effort into the marriage.

Activity: INDIVIDUAL AND COUPLE EVALUATION

Time: 10 minutes

Ask the couples as individuals to write answers to the following questions:

1. What expectations did you have for marriage when you were first married?

2. Which of those expectations have been fulfilled?

3. What are your expectations for marriage now? How have these changed over the years?

4. What were your spouse's expectations then? What are they now? How did you become aware of them?

5. What are three of your spouse's expectations now? How are you fulfilling them?

Ask the couples to sit face to face, not side by side, and to share their answers with each other. They will need to spread out in the classroom in order to have some privacy. During this time you should not go around and listen in. This is a private discussion between husband and wife. Those who are there without their spouses may meet in a group and discuss their responses to the questions. Give the couples at least 10 minutes to discuss these questions. They may need more time; you can decide how much time to allow by glancing around the room to see which couples are still intent in their discussion and which couples seem to be finished.

Activity: GROUP DISCUSSION

Time: 20 minutes

Divide the class into groups of six to eight each (three or four couples). Tell them that they will have approximately 10 to 12 minutes to discuss the following question: "What goals should a Christian couple have for their marriage?" (Use the transparency and show the question on the screen.) If the couples have time in their groups, ask them to list these goals in order of importance. Spend the remainder of the time having groups share their lists with everyone. Ask if others agree or disagree with each group's goals.

Activity: LECTURE

Time: 10 minutes

The importance of goals has been stressed by psychiatrist Ari Kiev of the Cornell Medical Center: "With goals people can overcome confusion and conflict over incompatible values, contradictory desires and frustrated relationships with friends and relatives, all of which often result from the absence of rational life strategies.

"Observing the lives of people who have mastered adversity, I have repeatedly noted that they have established goals and, irrespective of obstacles, sought with all their effort to achieve them. From the moment they've fixed an objective in their mind and decide to concentrate all their energies on a specific goal, they begin to surmount the most difficult odds."[1]

Goals give you a sense of direction. They are not what *will* be, but what you hope will be attained. Because they are future-oriented, they can lift us from some of the difficulties of our present situation. Our focus can be upon positive hopes to come. As Christians we live in the present and future. Scripture admonishes us to have purposes and direction for our lives. "Forgetting the past and looking forward to what lies ahead, I strain to reach the end of the race" (Phil. 3:13,14, *TLB*). "A man's mind plans his way, but the Lord directs his steps." (Prov. 16:9, *RSV*). Once we set goals, our steps can be directed by the Lord.

Goals will help you use your time more effectively, for they help you sort out what is important and what is not. If you know what you intend or need to do, it is much easier to keep from being sidetracked.

As we decide upon goals, we need to realize that a goal is an event in the future that is accomplishable and measurable. If I say that I want to be a good swimmer, I am stating a purpose. If I say that I want to be able to swim six laps in an Olympic-size pool by July first, I am stating a goal. (Write the sentence, "Spend two hours per week in direct, face-to-face communication with my spouse by the end of Feburary" on a transparency, large sheet of paper or chalkboard and underline the characteristics as you give them.)

Here are the characteristics of well-stated goals.

1. A goal should be stated in terms of the end result. Example: Spend two hours per week in direct, face-to-face communication with my spouse by the end of February.

2. A goal should be achievable in a definite time period. Example: Spend two hours per week in direct, face-to-face communication with my spouse *by the end of February*.

3. A goal should be definite as to what is expected. Example: Spend two hours per week in *direct, face-to-face communication* with my spouse by the end of February.

4. A goal should be practical and feasible. Example: Spend *two hours per week* in direct, face-to-face communication with my spouse by the end of February.

5. A goal should be stated precisely in terms of quantities where applicable. Example: Spend *two hours per week* in direct, face-to-face communication with my spouse by the end of February.

6. A goal should have one important goal or statement rather than several.

CONCLUSION

Remind the couples to complete chapter 4 in their text. Ask them to come early for the next session, which will take 70 minutes.

Close the session with prayer.

ALTERNATE SESSION

If you are using this curriculum in a weekend seminar or in a marital enrichment weekend, you may want to use the format suggested as an alternate session.

Activity: GROUP SHARING

Time: 10 minutes

Divide the class into groups of seven to ten. Tell them that each person will have one minute to tell the funniest thing that has happened to him in marriage. Be sure they limit their time. After the allotted time, depending on how many you have in each group, ask them to stop.

Activity: INDIVIDUAL EVALUATION

Time: 10–15 minutes

Distribute a copy of the Marriage Goal Wheel. You will need to make your own reproduction master and duplicate copies of the wheel in advance. The wheel should look like this:

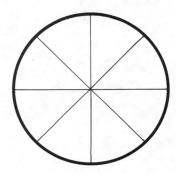

DIAGRAM 1

Ask each couple to write in between each of the eight spokes one goal that they have for their marriage. The goals should be summarized in a few words. Give the class plenty of time to complete this task. Then mention that most goals or objectives have several characteristics. A goal or objective should be realistic or attainable, and also measurable. That is, there should be a standard by which the couple can determine if the goal has been reached. Most goals have a deadline. Ask the couples to reconsider their goals in light of these criteria.

Now ask them to write their answers to these questions. Put the questions on a transparency and reveal them one at a time as you mention them.

1. Which are your four most important goals? Make a check beside them.

2. What is the order of their importance? List these four goals in order of importance.

3. If you had to give up two of your eight goals, which two would you be willing to do without? Mark them with a check.

4. Which of these goals do you think your spouse has written down? Write an "S" by them.

5. Which of these goals did you learn from your parents? Write a "P" by them.

6. Which of these goals do you feel God considers important? Write a "G" by them.

7. Choose one of your goals and explain why it will enhance or enrich your marriage. Why is it so important?

When the couples have finished answering the questions, ask them to put away their papers for now.

Activity: GROUP DISCUSSION

Time: 25 minutes

Divide the couples into groups of five or six. Ask them to decide what goals a Christian couple should have for their marriage relationship. (Allow 15 minutes.)

Then ask several of the groups to share their answers to the question, "What goals should a Christian couple have for their marriage relationship?" Ask them to expand on any that you feel are significant. If no one mentions a goal concerning money or financial security, ask, "Should a Christian couple have money or economic security as a goal? Wouldn't some consider such a goal unscriptural?" This goal is as important as any of the others because it reflects stewardship of God's gifts.

Activity: FACE TO FACE

Time: 10–15 minutes

Ask the couples to sit face to face and share their goals from the individual evaluation earlier, and their answers to the questions concerning their goals. After they have shared for several minutes, ask the entire group this question: "Setting goals is just one step. After goals have been established, what is the next step?" (One answer is, Determining the priority of the goals. Share with the group the procedure to follow in evaluating their goals. See chapter 4 of the text. If each person has a copy of the text, ask them to turn to it and read the steps.) The answer you are looking for is, *Developing a plan to reach the goal.* Have each couple select one goal and decide together the steps they will take to achieve that goal.

Activity: PRAYER

Time: 2–5 minutes

Ask the couples to pray together concerning their own lives and the accomplishment of the goal they have chosen.

Note

1. Ari Kiev, *A Strategy for Daily Living* (New York: Free Press, 1973), p. 3.

Ten Commandments for Married Couples

OBJECTIVES

1. To develop an ability to identify and fulfill the needs of a marital partner.

2. To identify guidelines for behavior that will enhance the marriage.

3. To develop steps that will lead to the implementation of positive behavior in marriage.

The material presented here and in session 6 will not fit in a one-hour session. Please read through this chapter and chapter 6 before proceeding. Suggestions for time allotments are given, but you may need to alter the time sequence to meet the needs of your group. Since all of these learning activities are so important you may want to give three sessions to these two chapters instead of two. If so, please alter the homework assignments.

ADVANCE PREPARATION

Have the overhead projector and the transparency "Ten Commandments for Married Couples" available. In this session we will cover the first five "commandments."

Activity: LECTURE

Time: 10 minutes

What type of needs do we have? Are we all alike in our basic needs, and can they all be satisfied in the same manner? There are many different ways to consider needs, and perhaps one of the easiest is to consider a simple structure called the "hierarchy of needs," developed by Abraham Maslow. He suggested that we have five basic needs. The lowest one in the hierarchy must be met before a person is motivated to reach for the next one. (These could be written on a chalkboard, large sheet of paper or on a transparency for everyone to see.)

The five needs, starting with the most basic, are:

1. Physical—air, water, food, whatever is necessary for life.

2. Safety—security, freedom from danger, confidence that our physical needs will be met.

3. Love and belonging—being wanted, cared about, listened to, accepted, understood, feeling important, receiving empathy.

4. Self-esteem—attention, respect, significance, value, achievement.

5. Self-actualization—creative potential, being autonomous, ability to give love *(agape)* and to fulfill one's potential or giftedness.

The first four needs are basically taking-in; they are self-centered. Before we can really reach the final need, we must pass through the first four stages. Our physical and personal needs must be met before we can become self-actualized.

Some of us enter adulthood with needs that were not adequately met in childhood, such as love, security, and belonging. Often these early unmet needs freeze into rigid behavior patterns and enter our marriage with us. Our adult behavior is then based upon these unmet needs from our childhood.

The amount of satisfaction you experience in your marriage is directly related to the fulfillment of your needs. One of the reasons people marry is their hope of satisfying their needs. How do you meet your needs? How much are you responsible to help your spouse meet his/her needs?

During the next two sessions we are going to study the ways we can develop the ability to identify and fulfill the needs of a marital partner. We are going to do this partly through the formation of "Ten Commandments for Married Couples."

Activity: GROUP DISCUSSION

Time: 45–50 minutes

Stage 1: Divide the class into groups of three couples. Their assignment as a group is to develop a list of 10 commandments for husbands and wives to follow in relationship to each other. Each person in the group should write his own copy of the list as ideas are shared. Allow 10 minutes for this activity.

Stage 2 will also take 10 minutes. Now ask the group to evaluate their commandments according to the following directions:

1. Indicate which of the commandments are normal and easy to carry out and which require considerable concentration and effort.

2. Indicate which of the commandments are the same as those you would use in normal interchange with friends and which are unique to marriage.

3. Indicate which of the commandments would meet a per-

son's need for love and security, self-esteem, and self-actualization (achieving one's potential or giftedness).

Stage 3. Evaluate these commandments on the basis of Scripture. Ask the group to discover Scripture portions to support these commandments. Allow 10 to 15 minutes for this stage.

Stage 4. Ask each group to choose one of its commandments and develop ground rules that would show how the commandment could be put into practice. Ask the group to be as specific as possible and develop step-by-step procedures. Allow 10 minutes for this.

Stage 5. Ask each individual to spend three minutes selecting (1) what he or she personally feels is the most important commandment and (2) what he or she feels her or his spouse would select. The couples then share the results together for two minutes.

Ask each group to give you the list of its 10 commandments, and post the various lists on the wall so all the couples can read them.

Activity: LECTURE

Time: 10 minutes

Each group has developed many excellent lists of commandments. Here are 10 suggested commandments others have developed. (Use the transparency for this presentation.) We will cover the first five commandments in this session.

1. *Cooperate with your spouse in every effort to improve and enhance your marital relationship.* You may find that one individual in a marriage may have more concern about upgrading the marriage than the other. One may feel the need to make a poor marriage good and a good marriage better. What have you to lose by cooperating with this positive desire?

You may learn more than you realize by reading and discussing a book together; by listening to a tape together; by subscribing to a marriage magazine and completing the assignments together; meeting every three months to evaluate, develop and implement goals; attending a marriage enrichment or marriage encounter weekend; or seeing a marriage counselor once a year for a marital evaluation and checkup! This last suggestion is just as important as going for your yearly physical. "You should be like one big happy family, full of sympathy toward each other, loving one another with tender hearts and humble minds. Don't repay evil for evil. Don't snap back at those who say unkind things about you. Instead, pray for God's help for them, for we are to be kind to others, and God will bless us for it" (1 Pet. 3:8,9, *TLB*).

2. *Give praise and appreciation instead of seeking it.* Too often an individual goes about seeking to have his own needs met first, and only when these have been satisfied does he attend to his spouse's needs. But you are most likely to see your needs by meeting the needs of your spouse. Philippians 2:4 says, "Let each of you esteem and look upon and be concerned for not [merely] his own interests, but also each for the interests of others" *(AMP).*

One practical way of being consistent in this demonstration of love is to make a commitment with yourself to give your spouse at least one compliment every day, and each week give one compliment that you have never given before. Too often we take for granted many of the day-to-day, simple behaviors that are so necessary. When is the last time a husband thanked his wife for the clean house, for laundered and ironed clothes or for meals properly prepared? When is the last time a wife thanked her husband for the energy he invests in his vocation, his interests in keeping up the home or car, etc.? (Ask for responses from the group to the question: "What are some of the loving behaviors that we take for granted on the part of our spouse?")

3. *Greet your spouse at the end of the day with love, affection and concern instead of complaints and demands.* What occurs during the first four minutes at the end of the day when you arrive home from work will set the tone for the remainder of the evening. How do you greet each other? Do you give more of a greeting to the dog than to your spouse? Do you take time to seek out your spouse when you arrive home, or is there silence, or "What a rotten day!" or "Wait until you hear what the kids did today!" Do you touch each other, ask about your spouse's needs or concerns or joys of the day?

Think for a moment about the typical way you greet each other. (You might want to ask participants to write out their descriptions.) How would your spouse describe it? What could you do differently that your spouse would appreciate and that would meet his/her needs? "Like apples of gold in settings of silver is a word spoken in right circumstances" (Prov. 25:11, *NASB*).

4. *Define areas of responsibility and decision-making, and base this upon ability giftedness.* Too often these areas are decided by who is male and who is female, and couples exist for years in dissatisfaction. Or the decisions are made by default. First Peter 3:1–9 gives us some advice on how to make this work. We will say more about this in the unit of study on decision-making.

Activity: GROUP DISCUSSION

Time: 25 minutes

5. *Discover your spouse's personal and unique needs and endeavor to meet them.* Divide the class into groups of six (three couples). Have each group form two concentric circles with the husbands in the inner circle. The wives are to listen without comment (verbal or nonverbal) while their husbands are sharing. This is called the Fishbowl Exercise. Give the husbands 10 minutes to discuss the following questions. You will have to judge how much time to allow for each one.

1. What typical needs do men have that they want fulfilled in marriage?

2. What specifically can a wife do to meet these needs?

3. What typical needs do women have that they want fulfilled in marriage?

Now ask the husbands and wives to switch places. Use the same guidelines for the wives as for the men's group. Give the wives 10 minutes to discuss these three questions:

1. What typical needs do women have that they want fulfilled in marriage?

2. What specifically can a husband do to meet these needs?

3. How do you feel about what the husbands said about their needs and what can be done to meet them?

CONCLUSION

When the discussion has concluded, ask the group what they learned through the experience.

Remind the couples to read and complete chapter 5 in the text before the next session.

Conclude with prayer.

SESSION SIX

Fulfilling Needs in Marriage

ADVANCE PREPARATION

1. Duplicate copies of questions about "In-Law Relationships" and the "Love Response Visualization Form."

2. Have the overhead projector and the two transparencies available ("Ten Commandments for Married Couples"; "Three Types of Love").

Time: 60 Minutes

Activity: LECTURE

Time: 15 minutes

In the last session we talked about the first five of "Ten Commandments for Married Couples." In this session we will cover commandments six through ten. **(Put the "Ten Commandments for Married Couples" transparency on the overhead projector.)**

6. *Learn the true meaning of love, especially agape.* Love is more than a feeling. It is an act of the will. Couples can choose to think loving thoughts and act in a loving manner. Too many overemphasize the emotional or feeling response type of love. One person described love in this way. "Love is a feeling you feel when you get a feeling you never felt before." Love is more than that, however. Let's consider the various types of love. **(Use the transparency for this portion of the presentation. As you present the practical, detailed examples of the three types of love, read each one slowly to the class, or write them on a transparency and reveal them one at a time.)**

We say that we marry for love, but what type of love? Let's look at three different types of love and their effect upon marriage.

Eros is need love. It is the love that leads to marriage. Most couples begin their marriage with a preponderance of eros love and a minimum of the others. Eros is necessary for marriage to succeed. Often it begins in attraction. This is illustrated in Diagram 2.

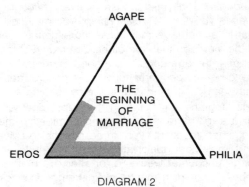

DIAGRAM 2

After marriage the eros or excitement phase begins to diminish, as Diagram 3 shows. We need to remember that a marriage cannot be sustained by eros alone.

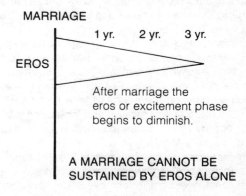

DIAGRAM 3

In many marriages *agape* and *philia* remain at a low level and eros has receded. The passion and excitement, which were the mortar holding the marriage together initially, are no longer there as we see in Diagram 4. At this point many couples begin to question, "Why am I married? Was I ever in love in the first place?"

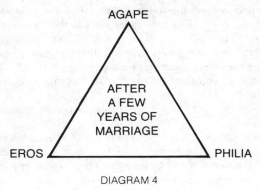

DIAGRAM 4

But this need not be the pattern for Christian marriages. If individuals would put forth effort to purposely increase philia and agape love, all three types of love would increase. The friendship love of philia can enhance and enrich both of the others. The agape love in turn can increase and enhance the others. Both agape and philia can enrich the eros love so it does not have to diminish as much as it usually does. It too can flourish if properly nurtured, and if so, the other types of love are reinforced. But all three must be given conscious effort.

Agape can keep the marriage going when eros and philia are low. (Show Diagram 5.)

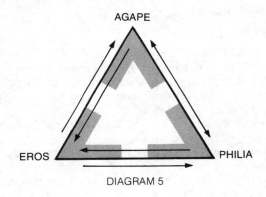

DIAGRAM 5

The following material, designed to give practical, day-by-day illustrations of these three types of love, has been taken from LeRoy Koopman's book, *How to Build a Happy Marriage*.[1] All of these types could be amplified further by using other material in the book or by using your own illustrations.

Eros. Eros is the love that seeks sensual expression. Eros is desire. Eros is a romantic love, sexual love. It is inspired by the biological structure of human nature. The husband and wife, in a good marriage, love each other romantically and erotically. Eros is:
■ the lingering touch of the fingers
■ the deep kiss
■ candles and music at dinner
■ the "I promise you" wink
■ a low whistle when she models a new dress
■ giving her a sheer negligee for her birthday
■ wearing it for him the same night

Ask for three additional suggestions from the couples.
Philia. In a good marriage the husband and wife are also friends. Friendship means companionship. Philia's companionship is many things:
■ being reasonably happy to go shopping with her
■ watching TV together and munching popcorn
■ feeling lonely when he's out of town
Ask for three additional suggestions from the couples.
Friendship also means communication. Philia's communication is many things:
■ sharing something you read in a book or magazine
■ reminiscing how you had to catch all the mice and remove all the bats before you could move into your first apartment
■ eating breakfast together without the morning paper
■ agreeing on the design of the new wallpaper for Jane's room
■ having the courage to tell her you don't like that dress she's trying on
Ask for three additional suggestions from the couples.
Philia is also cooperation. While eros is almost always a face-to-face relationship, philia is very often a shoulder-to-shoulder relationship. When there is philia, husband and wife are working together on something greater than both of them. They are finding their oneness, not directly in each other, but in their interest in a common cause. In eros each seeks fulfillment in the other; in philia they both seek fulfillment in one mutual goal.
Philia cooperation is:
■ weeding the tomatoes together
■ papering the kitchen wall
■ working out a new budget with the old income and the new inflation
■ washing and drying dishes together
Ask for three additional suggestions from the couples.
Here is a quote from another resource to help explain the friendship phase of marriage:
"And what is a friend? Many things...
"A friend is someone you are comfortable with, someone whose company you prefer. A friend is someone you can count on—not only for support, but for honesty.
"A friend is one who believes in you...someone with whom you can share your dreams. In fact, a real friend is a person you want to share all of life with—and the sharing doubles the fun.
"When you are hurting and you can share your struggle with a friend, it eases the pain. A friend offers you safety and trust... whatever you say will never be used against you.
"A friend will laugh with you, but not at you...a friend is fun.
"A friend will pray with you...and for you.
"My friend is one who hears my cry of pain, who senses my struggle, who shares my lows as well as my highs.
"When I am troubled, my friend stands not only by my side, but also stands apart, looking at me with some objectivity. My friend does not always say I am right, because sometimes I am not.
"My lover, my friend—this is what a marriage partner should be."[2]
Agape. Agape is self-giving love, gift love, the love that goes on loving even when the other becomes unlovable. Agape can keep erotic love alive or rekindle erotic love that has been lost. *Agape love is not just something that happens to you; it's something you make happen.* Love is a personal act of commitment. Christ's love (and hence the pattern for our love) is gift love. Christ's love for us is unconditional. Christ's love is eternal love.
Agape is kindness. It is being sympathetic, thoughtful, and

sensitive to the needs of your loved one. What is agape kindness? It is:

- being gentle when she burns the toast
- treating his case of the flu as if it were a combination of the eight most awful ailments even known to mankind
- squelching the urge to ask whether she's been eating more chocolates lately
- listening when she wakes up and wants to talk at 2:35 A.M.
- helping to put the children to bed, even during the fourth quarter of the TV football game

Ask for three additional suggestions from the couples.

Agape kindness is servant power. Kindness is love's willingness to enhance the life of another. It is the readiness to move closer to another and allow him to move close to you. Agape is trying to be content with those things that don't live up to your expectations.

What is agape contentment? It is:

- learning to live with less than perfection
- not making nostalgic comments about your mother's fine cooking
- using gentle encouragement instead of nagging insistence
- not complaining about eating at McDonald's instead of Caesar's

Ask for three additional suggestions from the couples.

Agape love is forgiving love. "Love forgets mistakes; nagging about them parts the best of friends" (Prov. 17:9, *TLB*). What is agape forgiveness? It is forgiving your partner for:

- squeezing the toothpaste tube wrong for the 837th time
- not remembering to pick up Freddy from his guitar lesson
- not having your shirt ironed on time
- having a relative like Uncle Howard

Ask for three additional suggestions from the couples.

Commandment number 7 is, *Don't attempt to change your spouse through criticism, pressure, or attack.* "Let us therefore stop turning critical eyes on one another. Let us rather be critical of our own conduct and see we do nothing to make a brother stumble or fall" (Rom. 14:13, *Phillips*). One of the best ways to bring about a change in another person is to change ourselves. The other person may change according to the change in us.

Learning to communicate concerns, needs, and frustrations openly and honestly in such a way that your spouse responds is possible. Change can and should occur. We need to remember that being asked to change is threatening and often we feel it is a risk. How do we feel when someone asks us to change? What do we say in response to him? (This area will be elaborated upon in the unit of study on change and crisis and in the unit on conflict resolution.)

Activity: GROUP DISCUSSION

Time: 10 minutes

8. *Exhibit the practical demonstration of 1 Corinthians 13:4–7 in your marriage relationship.* We have talked about love already, but let's consider another perspective on love. Distribute the "Love Response Visualization Form" to each person. Ask the couples to complete as much of this form as possible together. Then have them form groups and brainstorm suggestions together.

Activity: INDIVIDUAL WORK

Time: 15–20 minutes

9. *Give up any dependency that you have upon your parents,*

and don't criticize your spouse's parents. Read Genesis 2:24. The word *leave* actually means "abandon," "forsake," "cutting off." The ties are severed (in a positive sense). Many who marry have left home *physically but not emotionally.* (At this point distribute copies of questions about "In-Law Relationships" and ask the couples to individually write their answers to the questions. This will take five to ten minutes. Ask for some responses from the group. Suggest that husbands and wives share their answers together at home.)

1. What do you think children, after they marry, expect from their parents?

2. What do you think parents expect from their married children?

3. What did or do your parents expect? Make a list and then put a plus (+) by the items you feel are reasonable and can be fulfilled. Put a minus (−) by those you feel are not reasonable.

4. What needs do your parents have at this point in their lives? Which of these could you help fulfill?

5. What needs in your life are your parents presently fulfilling? Could your spouse help meet these needs?

6. How often do you see your parents or in-laws? Is this satisfactory?

7. Do you visit your in-laws on your vacation? If you do, do you consider this a "visit" or a "vacation"?

8. Do you spend Christmas or Thanksgiving with in-laws? If so, how do you feel about this?

9. Do you know how your spouse would answer these questions? (You may want to encourage the couples to read the book *In-Laws, Outlaws: Building Better Relationships* by Norman Wright [Harvest House]. This book deals with many of these and other in-law issues.)

CONCLUSION

Time: 3–5 minutes

Commandment number 10 is *Depend upon God's wisdom and God's Word for direction.* Have different individuals look up and read the following Scripture passages from the *New American Standard Bible:*

- "How can a young man keep his way pure? By keeping it according to Thy word" (Ps. 119:9).
- "Thy word have I treasured in my heart, that I may not sin against Thee" (Ps.119:11).
- "Make your ear attentive to wisdom, incline your heart to understanding" (Prov. 2:2).
- "For the Lord gives wisdom; from His mouth come knowledge and understanding" (Prov. 2:6).
- "Trust in the Lord with all your heart, and do not lean on your own understanding. In all your ways acknowledge Him, and He will make your paths straight. Do not be wise in your own eyes; fear the Lord and turn away from evil" (Prov. 3:5–7).
- "Acquire wisdom! Acquire understanding! Do not forget, nor turn away from the words of my mouth" (Prov. 4:5).

Remind the class to read chapter 6 in their text. They should bring their texts to the next session.

Conclude the session with prayer.

Notes

1. LeRoy Koopman, *How to Build a Happy Marriage* (Grand Rapids: Baker Book House, 1976), pp. 4–23.
2. Colleen Evans and Louis Evans, Jr., *My Lover, My Friend* (Old Tappan, NJ: Fleming H. Revell, Co., 1975), pp. 121, 122.

Marital Change and Stress

OBJECTIVES

1. To identify the effects of change and stress on an individual's life and marital relationship.

2. To determine how much stress each person has been experiencing during the past year.

3. To identify some of the reactions David, Job, and Elijah showed toward stress in their lives.

4. To identify and apply biblical teachings that can assist us during times of change.

ADVANCE PREPARATION

1. Read 1 Kings 18 and 19 three times in order to summarize the content.

2. Have available the overhead projector and the transparencies "Discussion Questions About Stress" and "Being 'In Christ.'"

3. Class will need to complete, in this session, the Holmes-Rahe Stress Test. Reproduce sufficient copies for this session.

Time: 60–65 minutes

Activity: LECTURE

Time: 10–15 minutes

We are in a constant state of change. Our bodies change, our beliefs change, our physical abilities change, and life around us changes. How do you respond to change? Do you look forward to it? Do you enjoy it or is it stressful?

If change produces stress in your life your health may suffer. Many medical doctors are concerned about the effects of stress on our bodies because when too much adrenaline—the hormone that is activated by stress—is secreted into our systems too frequently our health could be adversely affected. Too many changes too fast may tax our ability to handle change.

Stress-producing change doesn't have to be negative change. Even positive change results in adverse effects. Moving to a nicer and larger house, receiving a promotion, or achieving success may be followed by depression, especially if we have had our lives carefully regimented. These positive changes carry some sense of loss if familiar surroundings, friends, church and social activities have been left behind, and could be an overload for a while. After much emotional and physical effort is expended, there is exhaustion and feelings of inadequacy and uncertainty in the new position. Feelings of self-esteem can be undermined with a change to a new and better position.

In attempting to evaluate the effects of change, two medical doctors devised a stress test. *(Distribute Holmes-Rahe test to each person.)* Let's take the time right now to mark the events that have happened in your life during the past 12 months. Then add up the points. **(Give the couples time to complete the test.)**

According to the two doctors who devised the test, Holmes and Rahe, if your score is under 150 stress units, you have only a 37-percent chance of being sick within the next two years. If your score is between 150 and 300, the probability rises to 51 percent. And if your score is over 300, the odds are four to five (80 percent) that you will be sick during the next two years. The predicted sickness could be a physical illness or depression. Serious illnesses are often preceded by a cluster of life-changing events. Illness or depression does not have to occur, however. Several people have had scores of 400 or more without an adverse side effect. Why? Because they were aware of the potential problems of the stress and were aware of this test. They dealt with all of these changes, because they anticipated them and talked through the possible effects before they occurred.

Let's think about people in the Scriptures who experienced stress. What about Job? If Job had taken this test, what would his score have been? When we consider all that Job lost and all the changes that occurred in his life within a week, we see that he could easily have had over 700 points on this scale. Job experienced deep pain—both physical and emotional. Job did not curse God, but he cursed the day on which he had been born. He also said that the thing he feared most had befallen him: "For what I fear comes upon me, and what I dread befalls me" (3:25, *NASB*). He also said, "Though He slay me, I will hope in Him. Nevertheless I will argue my ways before Him" (13:15, *NASB*).

Look at your score. Even if it is low you may need to reaffirm Job's decision in your life.

Activity: GROUP BIBLE STUDY AND DISCUSSION

Time: 20–25 minutes

Summarize the contents of 1 Kings 18:1–17 for the couples.

Then divide them into groups of six. Ask them to read 1 Kings 18:38–19:18 to themselves in their groups. Then show the transparency "Discussion Questions About Stress," and ask the couples to discuss the questions on the screen.

1. What were the stress factors in Elijah's life?

2. What were the causes of his depressions?

3. How did God respond to Elijah, and what are the implications for us when we are under stress?

4. What are some of the stresses that we bring on ourselves?

5. What are some of the stresses over which we have little control?

6. What guidelines do the Scriptures give us for dealing with changes in our life?

Ask for several responses toward the end of your time for this session. (If the couples need some passages to consider, suggest Ps. 37; Rom. 12:2; 2 Cor. 4:8–12; and 1 Pet. 1:13.)

Activity: LECTURE

Time: 25 minutes

Elijah is a classic example of a man who experienced a great deal of stress and depression. Elijah's despondency moved him to the point of even wanting to die (1 Kings 18–19). Elijah was an example of a man who misinterpreted a situation and saw only certain elements of it. He had misconceptions concerning himself, God, and others. This happened partly because of his tremendous emotional and physical exhaustion.

Elijah had an intense emotional experience in the demonstration of God's power. Perhaps he expected that everyone would turn to the true God and was disappointed when Jezebel was still so hostile. He was physically exhausted by the encounter on Mount Carmel and his 20-mile race before the king's chariot. When Jezebel threatened his life, he became frightened. He probably spent time dwelling upon the threat (and forgot about God's power which had just been demonstrated). Fearing for his life, he left familiar surroundings and cut himself off from his friends.

All of these factors led to the depression. The distortion of his thinking is evident in his idea that he was the only one left, the only one who was faithful to God. He was convinced that the whole world was against him. Possibly he had some self-pity, which helped him lose perspective. His stress reaction to a positive event on the mountain, and physical exhaustion, all contributed to his depression.

An encouragement to us is the graciousness of the Lord that is evident in this account. Nowhere did God berate Elijah for being depressed or tell him to confess his depression as a sin! Instead He sent an angel to minister to Elijah. The prophet slept and was given food. God allowed Elijah to "get everything off his chest." The prophet told God his complaint and concern. Then God did two things: He pointed out to Elijah the actual reality of the situation; and He asked Elijah to get into action—He gave him an assignment.

This account of Elijah helps us see the various causes of depression; it also gives us insight as to how God responds to a depressed person. God is aware of our stress and reactions and we do not stand alone.

Let's look at some of the passages that may help us as we go through change and stress in our life. Fear and worry are common elements during change because the unknown or unexpected bothers us. And when we as individuals are bothered, our marriage can be affected. In order for our partner to help and support us at this time, we need to share with him/her what is going on in our life. We cannot expect him/her to be a mind reader.

"Psalms 37:1 *KJV* begins with the words *Fret not...* and those two words are repeated in later verses. The dictionary defines fret as 'to eat away, gnaw, gall, vex, worry, agitate, wear away.' One of the delights of the Word of God is that when God says not to do something or to stop something, a positive substitute is provided. This psalm makes four positive suggestions regarding worry or fretting. Verse three states *Trust in the Lord...The Amplified Bible* renders the word trust as *lean on, rely on, and be confident.* This is a matter of not attempting to live an independent life and cope with difficulties alone. It means going to a stronger source for strength. Verse four tells us to *delight* yourself in the Lord. Delight means to rejoice in God and what He has done for us. Let God be and supply the joy for your life.

"Committing your way to the Lord is another one of the alternatives to fretting. Commitment is a definite act of the will and it involves releasing your worries and anxieties to the Lord. It is a complete flinging of one's self upon the Lord with no conditions or holding back. It means to dislodge the burden from your shoulders and lay it on God. It is part of the life of faith wherein we give ourselves to God, simply relying upon what we know of God as expressed in Scripture and not depending upon circumstances that we understand or can see visually.

"The final suggestion is to rest in the Lord and wait patiently for Him. This word *rest* has a rich meaning. The Hebrew means 'to cease, be silent, or submit in silence to what He ordains.' But this involves a readiness and expectation for what God is going to bring and do in your life.

"The principle in this psalm is: *Give up fretting and replace it with trusting God, relying upon Him to provide and expect Him to do so. Release yourself completely to Him.*

"The results of prayer as a substitute for worry can be vividly seen in two Old Testament passages. In Psalms 34, *RSV*, David, who was undergoing a crisis in his own life, begins: *I will bless the Lord at all times; his praise shall continually be in my mouth.* David had just escaped from the Philistines who had captured him. He had faked the role of a madman knowing that they would release him rather than kill him. He then fled and hid in the cave of Adullam along with four hundred men who are described as men who were in distress, discontented, and in debt. In the midst of all this David wrote this psalm of praise. He did not say he would sometimes praise the Lord, but would do so *at all times.* No exception! This must have been a fearful time for David, knowing that the enemy was still after him. In verse four, *RSV*, he says, *I sought the Lord, and he answered me, and delivered me from all my fears.* David had neither fear, worry, nor anxiety. He prayed and gave the problem over to God who lifted it away. Nor did David turn around and take these cares back after he had deposited them with the Lord. He gave them up. Too many people give their burdens to God with a rubber band attached. As soon as they stop praying the problems bounce back. Some people pray, *Give us this day our daily bread,* and then when they are through praying begin to worry where their next meal is going to come from.

"Another factor to remember here is that God did not take David away from his problem. He was still in the cave with four hundred disgruntled men and he was still hiding. God does not always take us out of a problem situation but He gives us the peace that we are seeking as we proceed through that experience. It happened to David and it happens today for those who pray, unload their cares on God, and leave them there."[1]

Our hope is based on many elements. It is based on the sovereignty of God. It is based on our relationship with Jesus Christ. He challenges us to live our life to the fullest in the midst of any difficulty. Jesus does not call us out of the world but into the midst of its struggle and pain. Our hope is built upon the fact that we are in Christ. Have you ever considered the extent to which we are in Christ? Being in Christ means that we can grow into a deeper communion with Him. It means that our whole life is surrounded by Him. And we need to recall this to our active memory. The Scriptures speak of being in Christ in this way (use the transparency):

Romans 3:24	Redemption in Christ
Romans 6:3	Baptism in Christ
Romans 6:11	Eternal life in Christ
Romans 6:23	The love of God in Christ
Romans 12:5	Being one body in Christ
1 Corinthians 1:2	Sanctification in Christ
1 Corinthians 15:18	Asleep in Christ (in death)
2 Corinthians 5:19	God in Christ
Galatians 2:4	Freedom in Christ
Galatians 2:17	Justification in Christ

Change is a part of our life. Some of it is planned for and some of it is unexpected. With our security based on Jesus Christ, it is possible to become more flexible and adaptable. We are not alone in what we do. Psalm 27:1 says, "The Lord is my light and my salvation; whom shall I fear or dread? The Lord is the refuge and stronghold of my life; of whom shall I be afraid?" (*AMP*).

CONCLUSION

Conclude your session by asking each person to think of which event would be the most upsetting to him if it were to occur. Then ask each one to consider something in his own life right now that is stressful or troubling him. Ask for several prayer requests. Ask the class to remember these in prayer during the week.

Ask couples to complete chapter 7 and read chapter 8 in their text before the next session. In addition, ask them to make a list of events that have been especially upsetting to them. They should bring their list to the next session.

Close in prayer.

Note

1. H. Norman Wright, *The Christian Use of Emotional Power* (Old Tappan, NJ: Fleming H. Revell, 1974), pp. 64–66.

Coping with Major Crises

OBJECTIVES

1. To identify the normal and abnormal stages of grief when someone has experienced a loss.

2. To identify ways of ministering to another person at a time of loss and grief.

3. To develop an awareness of what a person experiences during loss.

ADVANCE PREPARATION

1. Duplicate copies of the form, "Grief and Ministry," for each person.

2. Have the overhead projector and the two "Grief" transparencies available for this session.

Time: 60 minutes

Activity: DISCUSSION GROUPS

Time: 10–15 minutes

Divide the class into groups of three couples. Ask them to share with one another from their homework assignment their list of upsetting events and how these compare to the list of the 25 most distressing events compiled by Eugene S. Pakyel. Ask them to share their responses to the first "What Do You Think?" section in chapter 8 concerning changes in their spouse, and then to share their responses to the various stages that we go through when we experience a loss.

Activity: LECTURE AND INTERACTION

Time: 25–35 minutes

Distribute copies of "Grief and Ministry" to each person.

Often when a person knows of an impending loss or radical change in his life, he goes through a bargaining stage. A typical example of this is when a person becomes aware that he is terminally ill. Bargaining is part of his normal reaction. "Spare me, Lord! Let me recover and be filled with happiness again before my death" (Ps. 39:13, *TLB*) is the prayer of so many people at this time. The person makes promises: "If I can get well then I will serve the Lord more than ever" or "If only I can live until June to see my son get married..." Then, if he lives that long, he says, "If only I can live to see my grandchildren," and the bargaining goes on and on.

This stage usually lasts only a brief period of time, but it can be intense while it lasts. Hezekiah, a man noted in the Old Testament, was told by the Lord, "Set your affairs in order, for you are going to die; you will not recover from this illness" (Isa. 38:1, *TLB*). When he received the news he turned his face to the wall and bargained with God. He reminded God of how he had served and obeyed Him and then broke down with great sobs (see Isa. 38:3). Hezekiah's prayer was heard by God, and he was given 15 more years to live.

His response to this experience is recorded in Isaiah 38:17–20: "Yes, now I see it all—it was good for me to undergo this bitterness, for you have lovingly delivered me from death; you have forgiven all my sins. For dead men cannot praise you. They cannot be filled with hope and joy. The living, only the living, can praise you as I do today....Think of it! The Lord healed me!" (*TLB*). Not everyone is healed, however; and other problems and difficulties do not always disappear when we plead.

What is grief? (Ask each person to spend one minute talking with another member of the group in defining grief. Have them describe the feelings and how a person might act. Ask for several responses after one minute.)

Grief over the death of a loved one is an extreme loss. We will consider this type of grief in this session for several reasons:

1. From this consideration we can see how we might respond to any type of loss.

2. We can learn how to help another person at a time of loss.

3. Most of us will experience this grief at some time in our life.

Grief is tears, an overwhelming sense of loss, a desire to be alone or to have social contacts severed or restricted. During this time some might even question God's wisdom or love. Some have feelings of guilt. Some have reactions such as "Why didn't I—"; "If I had treated him better" or "If I had sought help earlier" or "If I had found a better doctor or hospital this might not have happened."

The first response is a shattering, devastating shock that comes with the news of the death. This shock is followed a month or so later by intense suffering and extreme loneliness. Sometime during the first or second year there is a slow, gradual strengthening and healing of the mind and emotions. For most people, the grief process can take up to two years. With other losses and changes, the amount of time varies.

How do most of us respond to those who are bereaved? We continue to pray for them for two or three weeks. We may continue to show them concern in tangible ways such as cards, phone calls, taking an occasional meal to them for two or three months. But at the time when they need our support the most, many of us discontinue our ministry. It might be a good idea for churches to develop a program of ministry wherein 12 families would commit themselves for a period of two months each to minister to the bereaved over the two-year period of time and thus help them through the hurt process. Cards, phone calls, inclusion within their family activities, helping them feel useful and productive, etc., would be a part of sharing their concern.

(At this point, ask the couples what they would do if a couple they knew were having a crisis such as illness, loss of a job, severe marital conflict, or financial problems. The couple has not asked for help. What should we do? What can be done?)

The stages of grief that people pass through are normal and can be immediate or postponed. *People in mourning should be encouraged to do their grief work.* (This is explained in detail later.)

(From your own experience and reading, you may want to expand each of these stages. Use the transparency.)

Stage 1: Shock and crying. We should not deny bereaved persons this outlet, for it is normal. Some uninformed and mistaken Christians have made comments such as, "Stop your crying. After all, your husband is with the Lord now." Such comments are not helpful and are quite insensitive. Psalm 42:3 states, "My tears have been my food day and night" (*NASB*). Let the person cry. Read also Psalm 38:17 and 2 Samuel 18:33.

Stage 2: Guilt. This is almost a universal phenomenon. Statements or reactions such as, "If only—"; "Why didn't I spend more time with him?" and "Why didn't we call in another doctor?" are often made. In the loss of a job or house or opportunities we ask, "Why didn't I—?"

Stage 3: Hostility. A bereaved person might be angry at the doctors for not doing more, angry at the hospital staff for not being more attentive, and angry at the person who died. A husband might react by saying, "Why did she die and leave me with three children to care for?" Then guilt and remorse sink in because of this spontaneous feeling. People are helped by knowing that these reactions are normal. These feelings should be expressed. In Job 7:11 we read, "Let me be free to speak out of the bitterness of my soul" (*TLB*).

Stage 4: Restless activity. The bereaved begin a lot of activities but lose interest and switch to another project. It is hard for them to return to their regular routines.

Stage 5: Usual life activities lose their importance. This loss of importance brings on further depression and loneliness. Their usual activities were important only because they were done in relationship with the deceased.

Stage 6: Identification with the deceased. The bereaved person may continue the projects or work of the deceased. A wife may carry on her husband's unfinished hobby. A husband may continue to add to the house, which had really been his wife's

project. He begins to do what the other person did and he does it according to the former spouse's style. In some cases people begin having pains where the deceased experienced symptoms. If the husband's back hurt extensively, the wife may find that her own back starts to ache. But all of this is just part of the identification process.

Granger Westberg suggested, in his book *Good Grief,* that there are 10 stages of grief that the normal person must pass through:[1]

1. *Shock.* Shock is our temporary anesthesia, our temporary escape from reality. How do we help at this point? Be near the person and available to help, but do not take away from the person what he can do for himself. The sooner he has to make some decisions and deal with the immediate problem the better off he will be.

2. *Emotional release.* Encourage the person to cry or talk it out.

3. *Depression and loneliness.* Be available to the person and let him know that whether he can believe it or not this stage will pass too. In the midst of this loneliness, one may feel isolated from God. Job cried out, "Oh, that I knew where to find God!" (23:3, *TLB*). He was in darkness and could not find God. He had not lost his faith in God, but he admitted that from the depths of his soul, he had no idea where God was. He was in blackness. He also said, "Behold, I go forward, but he is not there; and backward, but I cannot perceive Him; when He acts on the left, I cannot behold Him; He turns on the right, I cannot see Him" (23:8, 9, *NASB*). But verse 10 gives the note of triumph: "But He knows the way I take." God knows exactly what is going on, and He knows exactly where we are.

4. *Distress.* There may be some symptoms of distress. Some of these could be due to repressed emotions.

5. *Panic* about ourselves or the future may set in. This can come because of the death being ever present in our mind.

6. *Guilt.* We have a sense of guilt about the loss. The person needs to be able to talk through these feelings with another person.

7. *Hostility and resentment.*

8. *Inability to return to usual activities.* Unfortunately, people tend not to talk about the deceased. They may remember an important time in the person's life or a humorous incident, but they refrain from talking about it in the presence of the remaining partner. And yet if they were to do so, they would probably find a positive response. In fact, the person may express gratitude that they talked about his loved one in this way. He is aware that those around him are very cautious about what they say, but fond remembrances are healthy.

9. *Hope.* Gradually, hope begins to return. Rabbi Joshua Liebman, in his book *Peace of Mind,* wrote an excellent chapter on "Grief's Slow Wisdom," which speaks most effectively to this temptation not to return to usual activities. Liebman said, "The melody that the loved one played upon the piano of your life will never be played quite that way again, but we must not close the keyboard and allow the instrument to gather dust. We must seek out other artists of the spirit, new friends who gradually will help us to find the road to life again, who will walk that road with us."[2]

10. *Struggle to affirm reality.* The final stage is the struggle to affirm reality. This does not mean that the person becomes his old self again. When one goes through any grief experience, he comes out of it a different person. Depending on his response, he can come out a stronger or weaker individual.

(At this point you may want some members of the group to share with the others their experience with grief when they lost a loved one. Ask them to remember what was helpful to them and what was not. Ask them about their feelings when they experienced other types of loss.)

A person should be encouraged to complete his grief work. What does this mean? Grief work means: (1) emancipating or detaching oneself from the deceased (read 2 Sam. 12:33); (2) adjusting to life without the deceased; and (3) making new relationships and attachments.

Grief work is the reviewing by the bereaved of his life together with the deceased. This involves thinking about the person, remembering dates, events, happy occasions, special occasions, looking at photos, and fondling trophies or items important to that person. In a sense, all of these activities are involved in the process of psychologically burying the dead.

We tend many times to deny the person his opportunity for grief work. We may come into the widow's home and find her looking at pictures in her husband's workshop and crying. How do we usually react? Perhaps we say, "Let's go do something else and get your mind off this." But it would be better if we could enter her world of grief and feel with her and perhaps cry with her. Romans 12:15 states that we are to "weep with those who weep" (NASB).

Tears are all right. Joyce Landorf said, "We must not be ashamed of our tears. Jesus wept on hearing of his friend Lazarus' death (even though He knew He was about to give Lazarus a remission from death!). To weep is not to be guilty of a lack of faith, nor is it a sign of hopelessness. Crying is a natural part of the grieving process."[3]

When grief is not expressed, there is a higher degree of what we call psychosomatic reactions such as ulcerated colitis, hypertension, etc. During the time of grief work, a person may show irritability and some strained interpersonal relationships. This is normal.

What can we say or do at this time of grief?

Begin where the bereaved person is and not where you think he should be at this point in his life. Do not place your expectations for behavior upon him. He may be more upset or more depressed than you feel he should be, but that is his choice.

Clarify his expressed feelings with him. You can do this by restating his words in your own words. Help him surface his emotions. You might say, "You know, I haven't seen you cry for a week. If I were in your situation, I would probably feel like crying." If the person is depressed, be near him and assure him that it will pass in time. He probably will not believe you and could even ask you to leave. Do not be offended by this.

Empathize—feel with him.

Be sensitive to his feelings and don't say too much. Joe Bayly gave this suggestion: "Sensitivity in the presence of grief should usually make us more silent, more listening. 'I'm sorry' is honest; 'I know how you feel' is usually not—even though you may have experienced the death of a person who had the same familial relationship to you as the deceased person had to the grieving one. If the person feels that you can understand, he'll tell you. Then you may want to share your own honest, not prettied-up feelings in your personal aftermath with death. Don't try to 'prove' anything to a survivor. An arm about the shoulder, a firm grip of the hand, a kiss: these are the proofs grief needs, not logical reasoning. I was sitting, torn by grief. Someone came and talked to me of God's dealings, of why it happened, of hope beyond the grave. He talked constantly, he said things I knew were true. I was unmoved, except to wish he'd go away. He finally did. Another came and sat beside me. He didn't ask leading questions. He just sat beside me for an hour and more, listened when I said something, answered briefly, prayed simply, left. I was moved. I was comforted. I hated to see him go."[4]

Don't use faulty reassurances with the person, such as, "You'll feel better in a few days," or "It won't hurt so much after awhile." How do we know that?

Remember not to give up helping the person too soon. The grief has been described in this way: "It seems when the initial paralyzing shock begins to wear off, the bereaved slowly returns to consciousness like a person coming out of a deep coma. Senses and feelings return gradually, but mingled in with the good vibrations of being alive and alert again is the frightening pain of reality. It is precisely at this time when friends, assuming the bereaved is doing just fine, stop praying, stop calling, and stop doing all those little kind things that help so much. We need to reverse this trend. In fact, we must hold the bereaved person up to the Lord more during the first two years of grief than in the first two weeks."[5]

A bereaved person needs:

Safe places. He needs his own home. Some people prefer to withdraw because their home reminds them of loss, but giving up the home and moving creates more of a loss. A brief change may be all right, but familiar surroundings are helpful.

Safe people. Friends, relatives, and minister are necessary to give him the emotional support he needs. It is better to visit the person four times a week for 10 minutes than to come once a week for an hour. This is more of a continual support without becoming exhaustive.

Safe situations. Any kind of safe situation that provides the bereaved person with worthwhile roles to perform benefits him. They should be uncomplicated and simple, and should not be likely to create anxiety. One pastor called upon a home in which the woman had just lost her husband. He could tell that people had been coming in and out all day long and that she was tired of receiving them and their concern. As he came in he said, "You know, I've had a tiring day. Would it be too much to ask you to make me a cup of tea or coffee?" She responded and fixed the coffee. When he was leaving she said, "Thank you for asking me to make you the coffee. I started to feel worthwhile and useful again."

Perhaps what we need in order to be able to minister to others is a clear understanding of what death is. For the Christian, death is a transition, a tunnel leading from this world into the next. Perhaps the journey is a bit frightening because we are leaving the security we feel here for the unknown, but the final destination will be well worth the present uncertainty.

Activity: GROUP DISCUSSION

Time: 10 minutes

Ask the group to divide into triads (spouses should not be together) and discuss how this information and these principles could be applied to their own lives to help them adjust to loss and change, and also to help them minister to others. Ask them to pray together in their groups.

CONCLUSION

Close the session by reading the following dedication written

—continued on page 30

Determining Who Makes Decisions

OBJECTIVES

1. To identify factors involved in making marital decisions.

2. To assist couples in identifying skills and strengths in each person to be used in decision-making.

3. To identify decisions that need to be made in the future.

4. To identify a biblical basis for decision-making.

ADVANCE PREPARATION

1. Duplicate the "Your Percentage of the Decision Analysis" form.

2. Have the transparency "Decision-Making in Marriage" and the overhead projector available.

Time: 60 minutes

Activity: INTRODUCTORY LECTURE AND INDIVIDUAL EVALUATION

Time: 15 minutes

All couples develop a style of making decisions. Some styles are effective; some are self-defeating. For many couples, decision-making is one of the most unenjoyable and even painful aspects of marriage. How you make decisions in your marriage determines whether this pillar is strong and supportive or is weak and contributing to an eventual deterioration of your marriage. (Read the following questions, and ask the couples to write their answers. Use the transparency.)

1. In which areas do you feel most comfortable making decisions? Why?

2. In which areas do you feel most comfortable about your spouse making decisions? Why?

3. Which decisions are husbands more likely to make, and which decisions do they prefer their wives make?

4. Which decisions are wives more likely to make, and which decisions do they prefer their husbands make?

In the book *The Mirages of Marriage,* Don Jackson and Richard Lederer state that the failure of couples to identify, determine, and mutually assign areas of competence and responsibility and determine who is in charge of what is one of the most destructive omissions in marriage.[1]

Certain tasks may appear quite clear-cut; many others are not. One myth that has been perpetuated over the years is the husband *must* be in charge of certain areas and the wife *must* be in charge of others. It's like saying certain tasks are male and certain tasks are female. This thinking keeps many couples from being able to use their unique talents and gifts adequately to enrich their marriage. For many evangelical Christians, this attitude is difficult to break away from.

If a person's temperaments, abilities, and training are not suited to an established cultural role, he·may become frustrated and question his abilities. He may also find devious means to avoid the responsibility and increasing conflict in his marriage. His spouse may question his abilities too.

Even though we may not want or be able to fulfill the established cultural roles, our relationship requires order and an assignment of roles. Proverbs tells us: "The plans of the heart belong to man, but the answer of the tongue is from the Lord" (16:1, *NASB*). "Commit your works to the Lord, and your plans will be established" (16:3, *NASB*). "The plans of the diligent lead surely to advantage, but everyone who is hasty comes surely to poverty" (21:5, *NASB*). This does not mean that role assignments and guidelines are locked into the marriage forever. They must be open to frequent revision.

One of the common complaints about establishing a marriage with a system of rules is that it is too rigid and unromantic. This system is thought to thwart the leading of the Holy Spirit in the relationship. Quite the contrary. Couples who overtly resist evaluating their marriage, setting goals, and determining the area of decision-making and roles are usually threatened because they feel insecure and inadequate. They also may not have developed a life-style of self-discipline. They may have to make some changes.

When a couple has guidelines for making decisions, their behaviors are predictable. Predictability develops trust in their relationship, which in turn allows freedom to develop exceptions to the rules when necessary. Assigning both authority and responsibilities creates flexibility in the relationship and thereby allows the couple to relax and give themselves to the tasks of enhancing their marriage and glorifying Christ.

What kind of trust do you want to develop as a couple? It is possible to develop negative trust as well as positive trust. If a spouse frequently does not live up to his promises or commitments, negative trust will develop. We can be predictable by not being trustworthy or dependable. This predictability, however, does not demonstrate love toward our partner. Spouses want the kind of predictability that creates positive trust.

Activity: GROUP DISCUSSION

Time: 20 minutes

Divide the class into groups of three couples each. Show the three questions for discussion on the transparency and ask the couples to discuss the questions in their groups.

1. What are 10 major decisions you as couples will probably have to make in the next 15 to 20 years?

2. How will you determine who is best qualified to make these decisions?

3. What are some scriptural guidelines you could use for making decisions?

After about 15 minutes, ask some of the groups to share what they have discovered.

Activity: COUPLE EVALUATION

Time: 10–15 minutes

Distribute copies of the ''Your Percentage of the Decision Analysis.'' Ask the couples to sit face to face and individually, without discussion, complete their forms. When everyone has finished, ask husbands and wives to exchange forms and compare answers. Ask them to spend several minutes discussing their responses to the questions. When most of the couples have finished or when you are running out of time, ask for feedback from the group.

Share with the couples the following thoughts:

It is commonly assumed that when a marriage contains a dominant spouse and a submissive spouse, the dominant one is the controlling one—in other words, the decision-maker. But in reality, the dominant one could be ineffective, because the submissive one probably controls the relationship through passive resistance, such as withdrawing, silence, and refusing to give an opinion.

Let's consider another factor about decision-making. Which of you makes the decisions more quickly? What effect does this have? In any relationship it is normal for one to be quicker and more decisive. This doesn't mean that the faster person is any more intelligent than the slower person.

The quicker spouse inserts his thoughts, his plan, his procedures into the discussion first and has a strong influence. He has the advantage, and thus the slower person tends to become even slower. He can't keep pace or catch up.

Activity: LECTURE

Time: 5–10 minutes

As you think about decision-making in your marriage, consider these four passages of Scripture. (You may want to have several people read the Scripture as you expound on their application to decision-making. These quotations are from the *New American Standard Bible.*)

Ephesians 4:23: "Be renewed in the spirit of your mind." Renewing the spirit of our mind means to renew that which gives the mind the direction and the contents of its thoughts. This passage speaks of God's Spirit influencing man's mental attitude. Do we ask for the leading of the Holy Spirit in our own thoughts as we consider decisions? Often our own desires and wants override His leading.

Colossians 3:17: "And whatever you do in word or deed, do all in the name of the Lord Jesus, giving thanks through Him to God the Father." Having our decisions reflect our relationship with Jesus Christ will build our relationship rather than cause dissension. This does not mean that we always give in to the other person's opinion if we feel that what we have to offer is correct and accurate. It does mean that perhaps we will discuss the issue as each person seeks to hear what the other has to offer.

Romans 12:4-10: "For just as we have many members in one body and all the members do not have the same function, so we, who are many, are one body in Christ, and individually members one of another. And since we have gifts that differ according to the grace given us, let each exercise them accordingly: if prophecy, according to the proportion of his faith; if service, in his serving; or he who teaches, in his teaching; or he who exhorts, in his exhortation; he who gives, with liberality; he who leads, with diligence; he who shows mercy, with cheerfulness. Let love be without hypocrisy. Abhor what is evil; cleave to what is good. Be devoted to one another in brotherly love; give preference to one another in honor."

Spiritual giftedness should be taken into consideration in decision-making, for each of us has something to offer in different realms. If couples would spend time discovering and implementing the spiritual gifts which they bring to their marriage relationship, they could accomplish much more in their marriage and for the Lord.

Verse 10 of Romans 12, as stated in *The Amplified Bible* reads, "Love one another with brotherly affection—as members of one family—giving precedence and showing honor to one another."

Philippians 2:3-5: "Do nothing from selfishness or empty conceit, but with humility of mind let each of you regard one another as more important than himself; do not merely look out for your own personal interests, but also for the interests of others. Have this attitude in yourselves which was also in Christ Jesus." (Ask how this passage could be applied to the area of decision-making in marriage.)

CONCLUSION

As you close this session, ask the couples to consider the following questions about a particular decision they may be facing. Reveal the questions one at a time on the transparency.

1. Is this decision based on your own needs or wants?

2. Is this decision best for your marriage relationship?

3. How will this decision glorify the Lord?

4. Who will benefit from this decision?

These questions may assist you in the decision-making process.

Remind the couples to read and complete chapter 9 in their books, and remind them to bring their books to the next class session.

Conclude with prayer.

Note

1. Don Jackson and Richard Lederer, *The Mirages of Marriage* (New York: W. W. Norton & Co., Inc., 1968), pp. 248, 249.

What Causes Conflicts and Quarrels?

OBJECTIVES

1. To clarify the meaning of conflict.
2. To identify causes of conflict.
3. To clarify and identify typical styles of handling conflict.
4. To identify steps to take in helping other couples handle conflict.

ADVANCE PREPARATION

1. Duplicate the "Conflict" and "The Counselor's Game" sheets for each member of the class.

Time: 55–60 minutes

Activity: LECTURE

Time: 5 minutes

Conflict is a normal part of life. All couples experience conflict in their marriage, whether they are Christians or not. The problem is not the conflict or the different beliefs or behaviors, but how a couple responds to the conflict. Let's first define the word. (Ask each person to turn to his spouse and spend one minute defining the word conflict. This activity is called "neighbor nudging." At the end of one minute, call time and ask for several responses.)

Here is a definition of conflict. The word can mean to strike together; a fight, clash, or contention; a sharp disagreement or opposition, as of interests, ideas, etc.; mutual interference of incompatible forces or wills.[1]

We know that both Paul and Jesus experienced conflict with others. Jesus was in constant conflict with the religious leaders of Judea. They wanted to defeat and destroy Jesus. They wanted to win over Him. (Read to the class John 8:1-11. Ask them what the conflict was and how Jesus responded to it. Ask what other ways Jesus could have used to respond to them.)

Activity: DISCUSSION GROUPS

Time: 10 minutes

Divide the class into groups of three couples. Distribute the "Conflict" form to everyone. Ask the groups to discuss what they feel are the typical causes of conflict between a married couple. Ask them to discuss also why these things create conflict. Every person can write his responses on the "Conflict" sheet. Give them about eight minutes and then ask for responses for the remaining time.

Activity: BRAINSTORMING GROUPS

Time: 8 minutes

Ask the groups to stay together. This time they will function as brainstorming groups. Ask them to list (not discuss) at least ten ways of coping or dealing with conflict. At the end of three minutes, call time and ask for their responses.

Activity: LECTURE

Time: 3–5 minutes

Share the following information with the class.

One of the traditional ways couples learn to deal with conflict is to suppress it—try to forget it, sweep it under the rug, or shrug it off. This so-called nice way has been equated with being Christian. Burying conflicts, however, only builds resentments, which drain you of energy and color your entire perception of daily life.

Another way couples handle conflict is to express their feelings unreservedly. For some couples, this approach resembles a war. Wave after wave of attack seems to mount, and the intensity increases. In time verbal garbage is thrown, computer memories are activated (and these would put an elephant's memory to shame), and total frustration is the end result. During this time each assumes the role of a skilled lawyer, eager not only to indict the other but to see him convicted (and in some cases hung!).

What does the Bible say about conflict? What does it say about quarrels? Are quarreling and conflict synonymous? Not really. Many conflicts are handled and resolved without quarreling.

A quarrel has been defined as verbal strife in which angry emotions are in control and the couple does not deal with the issue but instead attacks the other person. This behavior creates strain in their relationship. The Scriptures tell us not to be involved in quarrels: "It is an honor for a man to cease from strife and keep aloof from it, but every fool will be quarreling" (Prov. 20:3, *AMP*). "As coals are to hot embers, and wood to fire, so is a quarrelsome man to inflame strife" (Prov. 26:21, *AMP*). "Let all bitterness and indignation and wrath (passion, rage, bad temper) and resentment (anger, animosity) and quarreling (brawling, clamor, contention) and slander...be banished from you" (Eph. 4:31, *AMP*).

Activity: GROUP DISCUSSION

Time: 20–30 minutes

Distribute a copy of "The Counselor's Game" to each person. Divide the class into new groups of either three or four couples. Assign each group a different case to discuss and analyze. Tell the groups that when they arrive at a solution to the problem in their assigned case, to go to another case and begin working on that one.

Leave the last 5 to 10 minutes for reports of how they would help the individual or couple resolve their conflict. You will probably have a wide variety of responses. You do not have to give the final answer for any of the cases. Your job is to encourage the class to think about how they would resolve the conflicts of someone else. It would help to point out that in some of the cases they are hearing just one side of the story. It would also be helpful to have the person or couple with the complaint define what they mean by some of the words they are using.

CONCLUSION

As you conclude this session, ask the couples to read chapter 10 in their text. They should not read further, however. Remind them that they need to bring their text with them to class for the next session—this is crucial for the next session.

Conclude the session with prayer.

Note

1. James G. T. Fairfield, *When You Don't Agree* (Scottdale, PA: Herald Press, 1977), p. 18.

Coping with Major Crises

—continued from page 26

by John Powell in *The Secret of Staying in Love:* "This book is gratefully dedicated to Bernice. She has been a source of support in many of my previous attempts to write. She has generously contributed an excellent critical eye, a cultivated literary sense and especially a confident kind of encouragement. She did not help with the preparation of this book. On July 11 she received a better offer. She was called by the Creator and Lord of the Universe to join the celebration at the banquet of eternal life."[6]

Ask the couples to reread chapter 8 in their text as a homework assignment.

Notes

1. Adapted from Granger Westberg, *Good Grief* (Philadelphia: Fortress Press, 1962), pp. 11–52.
2. Joshua Liebman, *Peace of Mind* (New York: Simon & Schuster, 1946).
3. Joyce Landorf, *Mourning Song* (Old Tappan, NJ: Fleming H. Revell, 1974), p. 147.
4. Joe Bayly, *The View from a Hearse* (Elgin, IL: David C. Cook, 1969), pp. 40, 41.
5. Landorf, p. 145.
6. John Powell, *The Secret of Staying in Love* (Niles, IN: Argus Publications, 1974).

Dealing with Marital Conflict

OBJECTIVES

1. To help couples identify conflicts in their own marriage.
2. To help couples identify and acknowledge conflicts in their marriage for which they are primarily responsible.
3. To identify, clarify, and apply new methods of handling conflict.
4. To identify an individual's typical style of handling conflict and the effects of that style.

ADVANCE PREPARATION

1. Duplicate the "Conflict Analysis" form.
2. Have the "Five Styles of Handling Conflict" transparency and overhead projector available.
3. You will need a copy of *The Living Bible* for this session.
Time: 60 minutes

Activity: NEIGHBOR NUDGING AND INDIVIDUAL EVALUATION

Time: 10 minutes

Ask each person to turn to his neighbor and for one minute discuss the question, "What are the typical conflicts of married couples?" At the end of one minute ask for several responses.

Distribute a "Conflict Analysis" form to each person to complete by themselves without discussing it with their spouse or anyone else.

Activity: INDIVIDUAL ANALYSIS AND COUPLE FACE-TO-FACE DISCUSSION

Time: 15–20 minutes

Ask each person to answer this question individually:

I generally deal with conflict in marriage by (1) screaming, (2) pouting, (3) pulling the silent treatment, (4) sharing my feelings calmly, (5) trying to see it the other person's way, (6) ignoring it and hoping it goes away, (7) praying about it.

Ask class members individually to write down areas of conflict in their own marriage. Then ask them to indicate which of these they are personally responsible for creating or continuing.

Ask the couples to sit face to face. Before they begin talking to each other, read the following Scriptures from *The Living Bible:* Proverbs 13:18; 23:12; 25:12; 28:13. Ask them to begin sharing by having the husband say to his wife, "This is a conflict that I feel I am primarily responsible for." He tells of the conflict; then his wife suggests what could be done to resolve the conflict. The husband is not to give any defense, but only to ask questions if he needs clarification. After one conflict has been discussed sufficiently, the wife shares a conflict for which she is primarily responsible, and the procedure is continued. Continue until you feel that the group has had sufficient time for discussion.

Ask the couples how they felt during this time. Ask if this is the typical way in which they deal with conflicts at home. If not, why not? What is the difference? Allow the class time to express their thoughts and feelings.

This method has been used extensively in seminars and Sunday School classes for several years. For many couples, this new procedure is a definite breakthrough in developing new methods of handling conflict.

Activity: LECTURE AND EVALUATION

Time: 30 minutes

What choices do we have in dealing with conflict? There are five basic ways of dealing with marital conflict. (Show the first diagram on the transparency "Five Styles of Handling Conflict.") On this transparency we see a way of diagramming these.

The first way is to withdraw. If you have a tendency to see conflict as a hopeless inevitability and one in which you can do little to control, then you may not even bother trying. You may withdraw physically by removing yourself from the room or environment, or you may withdraw psychologically by not speaking, ignoring, or insulating yourself so much that what is said or suggested has no penetrating power. There are many who use the backing-off approach to protect themselves.

Winning is another alternative. If your self-concept is threatened or if you feel strongly that you must look after your own interests, then the winning method may be your choice. If you have a position of authority and it becomes threatened, winning is a counterattack. No matter what the cost, winning is the goal.

People employ many different tactics in order to win. Since married couples are so well aware of each other's areas of vulnerability and hurt, they often use these areas to coerce the other person into giving in to their own demands. "Winners" may attack self-esteem or pride in order to win. They may store up grudges and use them at the appropriate time in order to take care of a conflict. They may cash in old emotions and hurts at an opportune moment. The stockpiling approach is another form of revenge and certainly does not reflect a Christian's demonstration of forgiveness.

If winning is your style, answer the following questions:

1. Is winning necessary to build or maintain your self-esteem or to maintain a strong picture of yourself? People need strong self-esteem in order to find satisfaction in life and in their marriage. But what is the foundation upon which this is built? If one is insecure or doubtful, he often creates a false image to fool others and in the process confuses himself. To defer to another, to give in, or to lose a debate or argument is a strong threat to the person's feelings about himself, and thus he fights so that this will not happen. The authoritarian person is not usually as secure as the image he portrays. Deferring to another is a sign of a weakening of his position.

2. Is winning necessary, because you confuse wants with needs? The spouse who feels he needs something may be more demanding about getting it than if he just wants something. Do you really make a distinction between needs and wants? You may see something as a *need* in your life, but your partner may see it as a *want*. How do you know if something truly is a need?

A third approach to handling conflict is yielding. We often see yield signs on the highway; they are placed there for our own protection. If we yield in a conflict, we also protect ourselves. We do not want to risk a confrontation, so we give in to get along with our partner.

We all use this approach from time to time, but is yielding a regular pattern for you? Consistent yielding may create feelings of martyrdom or eventually may create guilt in our partner. We even find some individuals who need to "lose" in a marital conflict. This approach is a face-saving way of doing that. By yielding, you give the appearance that you are in control and are the one behaving in the "most Christian" way.

We learn to suppress or repress our anger and pile it up instead of doing what Nehemiah did when he heard of the mistreatment of the poor people. "I [Nehemiah] was very angry when I heard their cry and these words. I thought it over, then rebuked the nobles and officials" (Neh. 5:6,7, *AMP*). Some people gain as much from defeat as others do from winning.

Another method of dealing with conflict is compromising or giving a little to get a little. You have discovered that it is important to back off on some of your ideas or demands in order to help the other person give a little. You don't want to win all the time, nor do you want the other person to win all the time. This approach involves concessions on both sides and has been called the "horse trading" technique.

A fifth method is called resolve. In this style of dealing with conflicts, a situation, attitude, or behavior is changed by open and direct communication. The couple is willing to spend sufficient time working on the difference so that even though some of their original wants and ideas have changed, they are very satisfied with the solution they have arrived at. In this diagram

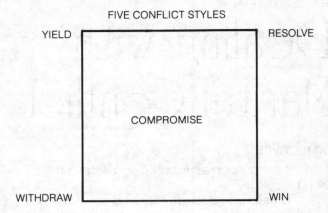

DIAGRAM 6

FIVE CONFLICT STYLES

YIELD — RESOLVE

COMPROMISE

WITHDRAW — WIN

you see the five ways of handling conflict. (Show diagram 6.)

Ask the class to turn to chapter 11 in their texts (find the page number in advance so you can tell them). Have them write their answers to the following questions:

1. Realizing that we may employ more than one method of handling conflict and may even use all five of the methods from time to time, indicate which style you use most of the time.

2. How does your style of reacting to conflict affect your marital relationship? How do you feel about it?

3. Which style does your spouse use most of the time?

4. Which style would your spouse say that you use most of the time?

The next question that arises is, Which method of handling conflict is best or ideal? Each of them has an element of effectiveness in certain situations. At times, compromise is not the best whereas winning may be. Yielding on certain occasions can be a true and pure act of love and concern. But the ideal style that we work toward is that of resolving conflicts.

Let's look at our diagram once again. (Show diagram 7 on transparency.)

You will notice that some new descriptive words have been added this time. When a person uses *withdrawal* as his normal pattern of handling conflict, the relationship suffers and it is difficult to see needs being fulfilled. This is the least helpful style

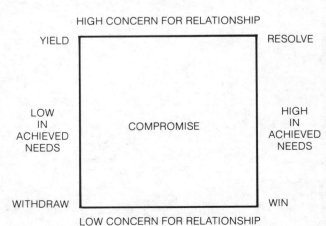

DIAGRAM 7

HIGH CONCERN FOR RELATIONSHIP

YIELD — RESOLVE

LOW IN ACHIEVED NEEDS — COMPROMISE — HIGH IN ACHIEVED NEEDS

WITHDRAW — WIN

LOW CONCERN FOR RELATIONSHIP

of handling conflicts. The relationship is hindered from growing and developing.

If this is your style, consider the reasons for this. It is not a demonstration of biblical submission or meekness. This method is often one of fear—fear of the other or of one's own abilities.

Winning achieves the individual's goal but at the same time sacrifices the relationship. A person might win the battle but lose the war. In a marriage, personal relationships are more important than the goal, and winning can be a hollow victory.

Yielding has a higher value because it appears to build the relationship, but personal goals or needs are sacrificed in yielding, which can breed resentment. Yielding may not build the relationship as much as some believe, because if the relationship was that important, a person would be willing to share, confront, and become assertive. What can be accomplished through resolution will build the relationship even more and shows a greater concern for the relationship than do other methods.

Compromising is an attempt to work out the relationship and the achievement of some needs. The bargaining involved may mean that some values are compromised. You may find that you are not very satisfied with the end result, but it is better than nothing. This could actually threaten the relationship. There may be a feeling of uneasiness following the settlement.

Resolving conflict is the ideal toward which couples are encouraged to work. The relationship is strengthened when conflicts are resolved, and needs are met on both sides. It takes longer and involves listening and accepting.

"A Christian response to disagreements includes a willingness to be patient in working out a solution.

"The willingness to exchange information, feelings, and ideas with one another leads to mutual understanding. Our first idea about a problem will not always be the same as our later understandings of it. As new ideas are expressed and the discussion develops, the issues may change."[1]

You may have changed in the process, but you are glad for the change. It is positive and beneficial. And change is possible and necessary! Because Jesus Christ is present in our life, we can give up our fears and insecurities. We can have a new boldness and courage to confront the issues of life and, in a loving manner, others around us. There are some who feel that change is impossible for them. But the Word of God says, "I can do all things through Christ which strengtheneth me" (Phil. 4:13, *KJV*).

What style of handling conflicts do we find in the Scriptures? Here are several passages of Scripture. Perhaps we can determine some of the styles as we look them up. Ask several people to look up Genesis 4 and read this passage silently. This is the account of Cain and Abel. Ask others to look up 1 Samuel 20:30-34; Matthew 15:10-20; Mark 11:11-19; Luke 23:18-25; John 11:11-19. Give them time to read and then ask the question, "What style of handling conflicts do we find in these passages?"

(Put "Conflict" transparency on overhead projector. Reveal only one line at a time.) This model has three steps that we can apply to a conflict. (Read through the three steps. This transparency usually elicits much laughter and response.) The alternatives to these three points are…(read A—H).

Here is another model of resolving conflict. (Go back to the "Five Styles of Handling Conflict" transparency and read "How to Resolve Conflicts.")

1. When a conflict arises, instead of demanding that you be heard, *listen carefully to the other person.* "He who returns evil for good, evil will not depart from his house" (Prov. 17:13, *NASB*). "This you know, my beloved brethren. But let every one be quick to hear, slow to speak and slow to anger" (Jas. 1:19, *NASB*). Any changes that one person wants to see in another must be heard and understood.

2. *Select an appropriate time.* "A man has joy in making an apt answer, and a word spoken at the right moment, how good it is" (Prov. 15:23, *AMP*).

3. *Define the problem.* How do you define the problem and how does the other person? You could suggest that you both stop talking and write down exactly what it is that you are trying to resolve.

4. *Define the areas of agreement and disagreement in the conflict.* Share with the other person first of all what you agree with him about, and then ask what he disagrees with you about. Writing the areas of agreement and disagreement on paper helps clarify the situation.

5. Here comes the difficult part. A few conflicts may be just one-sided, but most involve contributions from both sides. *Identify your own contribution to the problem.* When you accept some responsibility for a problem, the other sees a willingness to cooperate and will probably be much more open to the discussion.

6. The next step is to *state positively what behaviors on your part would probably help,* and be willing to ask for his opinion. As he shares with you, be open to his feelings, observations, and suggestions. Watch out for defensiveness!

CONCLUSION

As you conclude the class, ask the couples to answer the following questions in writing.

1. How will the presence of Jesus Christ in your life help you deal with conflict?

2. What one conflict do you want to resolve this week, and what will you do to resolve it?

Remind the couples to complete chapter 11 in their texts.

Close with prayer.

Note

1. Roy W. Fairchild, *Christians in Families* (Atlanta: John Knox Press, 1964), pp. 169, 170.

Learning to Forgive Completely

OBJECTIVES

1. To clarify and identify specifically what forgiveness is and what it is not.

2. To clarify class participants' attitudes concerning forgiveness.

3. To identify situations in which offering forgiveness is difficult.

4. To identify steps that will assist us in being forgiving of others.

ADVANCE PREPARATION

1. Duplicate the "Forgiveness Sentence Completion" form.

2. Have the "Forgiveness—What it Is, What it Isn't" transparency and overhead projector available.

Time: 60 minutes

Activity: DISCUSSION AND EVALUATION

Time: 10–15 minutes

As you begin this session, ask each person to take a minute and write his definition of forgiveness. Then ask for several responses. Distribute the sentence completion form and ask each person to finish the sentences by writing down the first response that comes to mind.

1. Forgiveness is...
2. When I forgive another, I feel...
3. It is most difficult for me to forgive when...
4. It is easiest for me to forgive when...
5. When I have been forgiven by another, I feel...
6. In order for forgiveness to occur I must...
7. The first time I experienced God's forgiveness I felt...
8. The main question I have concerning forgiveness is...
9. Forgiving myself is...
10. The Bible teaches that forgiveness is...

When everyone completes the form, divide the class into small groups of two couples each and ask them to discuss their responses.

Activity: DISCUSSION GROUPS

Time: 15 minutes

Divide the class into groups of three couples each. They will have the following questions to discuss:

1. What situations are the most difficult for married couples to forgive each other for?

2. What are the steps to take in forgiving each other? Let the couples know that they will have 10 minutes for their discussion. Spend the last five minutes having the various groups share some of their responses.

Activity: LECTURE

Time: 10 minutes

(Use the transparency "Forgiveness—What it Is, What it Isn't" as you proceed through this next section of material.) If we know Jesus Christ as Saviour, we have experienced God's forgiveness. Because we are in Christ, we have the capacity to forgive ourselves and thus are enabled to forgive others.

Paul spoke to us directly on this account: "Be gentle and forbearing with one another and, if one has a difference (a grievance or complaint) against another, readily pardoning each other; even as the Lord has freely forgiven you, so must you also [forgive]" (Col. 3:13, *AMP*).

The gradual erosion and total destruction of many marriages has come through lack of forgiveness. The desire to hold an event or action over another and continue to punish him erects a wall of difference and coldness. More than any other people, Christians have the capacity for forgiveness.

What is forgiveness? What is it not? Perhaps one of the best ways to discover what forgiveness is, is to consider what it is not. Forgiveness is not forgetting. God constructed us in such a way that our brain is like a giant computer. Whatever has happened to us is stored in our memory. We will always remember it.

There are, however, two different ways of remembering. One is to recall the offense or hurt in such a way that it continues to affect us and our relationship with another. It continues to eat away and bother us so that the hurt remains. Another way of remembering, however, simply says, "Yes, that happened. I know it did, but it no longer affects me. It's a fact of history, yet has no emotional significance or effect. It's there, but we are progressing onward at this time, and I am not hindered nor is our relationship hurt by that event." This is, in a sense, forgetting. The fact remains, but it no longer entangles us in its tentacles of control.

Forgiveness is not pretending. You cannot ignore the fact that an event occurred. Wishing it never happened will not make it go away. What has been done is done, and becoming a martyr and pretending ignorance of the event does not help the relationship. In fact, your lack of confrontation and reconciliation may encourage the other person to continue or repeat the same act or behavior.

Forgiveness is not a feeling. It is a clear and logical action on your part. It is not a soothing, comforting, overwhelming emotional response that erases the fact from your memory forever.

Forgiveness is not bringing up the past. It is so easy to bring up past offenses and hurts. There are some who have a trading stamp book with unlimited pages. For each hurt, they lick a stamp and paste it in. When the right time comes, they cash in those pages. Bringing up the past is destructive because:

- There is nothing you can do to change it.
- It takes you away from giving your energy to the present and future.
- It makes you responsible at this point for jeopardizing the marriage.
- Even if you were severely offended, by dwelling on the offense you place a continuing burden on your marriage.
- It denies your partner the opportunity to change for the better. This behavior also denies the presence and power of the person of Jesus Christ in a life!
- It does little to elevate you in the eyes of others. An indication of maturity is the desire and willingness to break loose of the past and move forward.

Forgiveness is not demanding change before we forgive. If we demand a change or demand proof of it first, we expose our own faithlessness and unwillingness to believe in the other person. He has already changed in a sense by coming and asking for forgiveness. The change is in his heart, but do we really trust that change?

Often, instead of complete forgiveness, we say, "I'll have to wait and see" or "Give me time." Time is often involved because forgiveness is a process and often does not occur instantaneously. We have to work through our feelings. But are we working through our feelings by ourself or waiting for definite signs of change on the part of the other person?

We don't want to risk being hurt again, so we are cautious and untrusting. This approach puts us in the role of a judge. The other person's change of heart has to be proved to us, and maybe our criteria of proof is so subjective that he can never measure up.

When forgiveness is lacking a strange bedfellow by the name of bitterness creeps in. Another word for bitterness is poison. It is poison to the person possessing it and to the relationship. The Word of God says, Let there be no more bitterness (see Eph. 4:31). Bitterness means that we have the desire to get even. But getting even costs. It can cost us in our bodies—ulcerative colitis, toxic goiter, high blood pressure, ulcers. These are just a few of the by-products.

Forgiveness is rare because it is hard. It will cost you love and pride. To forgive means giving up defending yourself. It means not allowing the other person to pay. It repudiates revenge and does not demand its rights. Perhaps we could say that it involves suffering.

"Forgiving is self-giving with no self-seeking. It gives love where the enemy expects hatred. It gives freedom where the enemy deserves punishment. It gives understanding where the enemy anticipates anger and revenge. Forgiveness refuses to seek its own advantage. It gives back to the other person his freedom and his future."[1]

Forgiveness is costly and is substitutional. "All forgiveness, human and divine, is in the very nature of the case vicarious, substitutional, and this is one of the most valuable views my mind has ever entertained. No one ever really forgives another, except he hears the penalty of the other's sin against him."[2]

Our greatest example of forgiveness is the cross of Jesus Christ. God chose the cross as the way of reconciliation. "For you have been called for this purpose, since Christ also suffered for you, leaving you an example for you to follow in His steps" (1 Pet. 2:21, *NASB*). "He himself bore our sins...on the tree" (1 Pet. 2:24, *RSV*). And we are called to forgive as God has forgiven us. "Be as ready to forgive others as God for Christ's sake has forgiven you" (Eph. 4:32, *Phillips*).

Activity: GROUP BIBLE STUDY

Time: 10 minutes

Divide the class into groups of two couples each. Ask them to look through Luke 15:11-32. Ask them to identify the specific indications of complete forgiveness that are found in this account. Ask them to discuss what it was that enabled the father to offer this forgiveness. Ask them also to identify the emotions described here and the behaviors that indicate love and forgiveness.

Activity: LETTERS ASKING FORGIVENESS AND PRAYER

Time: 10–15 minutes

During this last amount of time, ask each person to close his eyes and think about his own marriage relationship. Ask people to think of some way, large or small, in which they might have offended their marriage partner. Then ask each one to take a piece of paper and write a letter to his husband or wife, indicating this offense and asking for forgiveness. Give them sufficient time to write. Ask the couples to sit face to face and exchange letters, reading them silently. After the letters have been read, they can discuss or talk with each other.

CONCLUSION

Ask couples to spend time praying together, recommitting their individual lives and their marriage to the Lord.

For homework ask them to read chapter 12 in their text.

Conclude the session in prayer.

Notes
1. David Augsburger, *70x7: The Spirit of Forgiveness* (Chicago: Moody Press, 1970), p. 40.
2. James O. Buswell, Jr., *A Systematic Theology of Christian Religion* (Grand Rapids: Zondervan, 1962), 2:76.

Notes

Notes

Notes

MARRIAGE EVALUATION FORM

1. Common goals and values	1	2	3	4	5	6	7	8	9	10
2. Commitment to growth	1	2	3	4	5	6	7	8	9	10
3. Communication skills	1	2.	3	4	5	6	7	8	9	10
4. Creative use of conflict	1	2	3	4	5	6	7	8	9	10
5. Appreciation and affection	1	2	3	4	5	6	7	8	9	10
6. Agreement on gender roles	1	2	3	4	5	6	7	8	9	10
7. Cooperation and teamwork	1	2	3	4	5	6	7	8	9	10
8. Sexual fulfillment	1	2	3	4	5	6	7	8	9	10
9. Money management	1	2	3	4	5	6	7	8	9	10
10. Decision-making	1	2	3	4	5	6	7	8	9	10

To find your marital potential, *first* consider where your marriage could be. If both of you have together made all the progress you can possibly make in the area concerned, you would have 10 points. *Next*, where is your marriage now? Give yourself a score from 1 (lowest) to 10 (highest) that represents your present level of achievement. Add up the numbers—this is the percentage of your estimated potential you already have. Subtract this number from 100. The remainder is the percentage of your marital potential that you still need to appropriate.

WHAT IS YOUR OPINION?

AGREE   **DISAGREE**

□   □   1. Men have different expectations for a marriage relationship than women.

□   □   2. The Bible teaches that we should avoid people who get angry much of the time.

□   □   3. Men have different emotions than women.

□   □   4. Individuals who are committed Christians will have few conflicts in their marriage.

□   □   5. Most conflicts in marriage are not the problems but merely symptoms of other problems.

□   □   6. Disagreement over money matters is the number one cause of marital discord.

□   □   7. Women buy more on impulse than men.

□   □   8. Husbands should take the initiative to solve problems when they are between his mother and his wife.

□   □   9. Sometimes, to save a marriage it is necessary to accept irritating or irresponsible behavior on the part of the spouse.

□   □   10. Crusades to change a spouse's behavior usually backfire, so we should learn to be more accepting and simply pray about it.

□   □   11. Most in-law problems come from the mother-in-law, not the father-in-law.

□   □   12. In the case of an impasse on a decision that a couple needs to make, the husband should be the one to decide.

□   □   13. A decision for the family's good should have higher priority than that of the man's professional advancement.

□   □   14. The partner who is most dominant is the one who has more control and influence in the marriage.

□   □   15. If our mate does something that bothers us, we should let him or her know and try to change that behavior.

□   □   16. The person who yields in a conflict is demonstrating Christian love.

□   □   17. Couples should work toward compromises in their conflicts.

□   □   18. A married individual who finds it necessary to clarify his needs to his partner and tell him/her to meet them is married to someone who is insensitive and lacks perception.

IN-LAW RELATIONSHIPS

1. What do you think children, after they marry, expect from their parents?

2. What do you think parents expect from their married children?

3. What did or do your parents expect? Make a list and then put a plus (+) by the times you feel are reasonable and can be fulfilled. Put a minus (−) by those you feel are not reasonable.

4. What needs do your parents have at this point in their lives? Which of these could you help fulfill?

5. What needs in your life are your parents presently fulfilling? Could your spouse help meet these needs?

6. How often do you see your parents or in-laws? Is this satisfactory?

7. Do you visit your in-laws on your vacation? If you do, do you consider this a "visit" or a "vacation"?

8. Do you spend Christmas or Thanksgiving with in-laws? If so, how do you feel about this?

9. Do you know how your spouse would answer these questions?

LOVE RESPONSE VISUALIZATION FORM

1 Corinthians 13:4-7 gives the Bible's definition of love. These verses indicate that love consists of many elements—negative and positive. As you consider them below, give three creative examples of how each could be applied in your marriage. Be specific.

1. Suffers long—endures offenses, is not hasty, waits for the Lord to right all wrong.

    (1)

    (2)

    (3)

2. Is kind—not inconsiderate, seeks to help, is constructive, blesses when cursed, helps when hurt, demonstrates tenderness.

    (1)

    (2)

    (3)

3. Is not envious but content—is not jealous of another person's success or competition.

    (1)

    (2)

    (3)

4. Is not arrogant, but humble—is not haughty, but lowly and gracious.

    (1)

    (2)

    (3)

5. Is not boastful, but reserved—does not show off, try to impress, want to be the center of attraction.

    (1)

    (2)

    (3)

6. Is not rude, but courteous.

    (1)

    (2)

    (3)

7. Is not selfish, but self-forgetful.

    (1)

    (2)

    (3)

8. Is not irritable, but good-tempered.

    (1)

    (2)

    (3)

9. Is not vindictive or wrathful, but generous.

    (1)

    (2)

    (3)

10. Does not delight in bringing another person's sins to light, but rejoices when another person obeys the truth.

    (1)

    (2)

    (3)

11. Is not rebellious, but brave, conceals rather than exposes another person's wrongdoing to others.

    (1)

    (2)

    (3)

12. Is not suspicious but trustful, not cynical, makes every allowance, looks for an explanation that will show the best in others.

    (1)

    (2)

    (3)

13. Is not despondent, but hopeful, does not give up because it has been deceived or denied.

    (1)

    (2)

    (3)

14. Is not conquerable, but invincible—can outlast problems.

    (1)

    (2)

    (3)

HOLMES-RAHE STRESS TEST

In the past 12 months, which of these have happened to you?

EVENT	VALUE SCORE	EVENT	VALUE SCORE
Death of spouse	100 ☐	Trouble with in-laws	29 ☐
Divorce	73 ☐	Outstanding personal achievement	28 ☐
Marital separation	65 ☐	Spouse begins or starts work	26 ☐
Jail term	63 ☐	Starting or finishing school	26 ☐
Death of close family member	63 ☐	Change in living conditions	25 ☐
Personal injury or illness	53 ☐	Revision of personal habits	24 ☐
Marriage	50 ☐	Trouble with boss	23 ☐
Fired from work	47 ☐	Change in work hours, conditions	20 ☐
Marital reconciliation	45 ☐	Change in residence	20 ☐
Retirement	45 ☐	Change in schools	20 ☐
Change in family member's health	44 ☐	Change in recreational habits	19 ☐
Pregnancy	40 ☐	Change in church activities	19 ☐
Sex difficulties	39 ☐	Change in social activities	18 ☐
Addition to family	39 ☐	Mortgage or loan under $10,000	18 ☐
Business readjustment	39 ☐	Change in sleeping habits	16 ☐
Change in financial status	38 ☐	Change in number of family gatherings	15 ☐
Death of close friend	37 ☐	Change in eating habits	15 ☐
Change in number of marital arguments	35 ☐	Vacation	13 ☐
Mortgage or loan over $10,000	31 ☐	Christmas season	12 ☐
Foreclosure of mortgage or loan	30 ☐	Minor violation of the law	11 ☐
Change in work responsibilities	29 ☐		
Son or daughter leaving home	29 ☐	TOTAL	___

GRIEF AND MINISTRY

Stages of Grief

1. _____ and _____
2. _____
3. _____
4. Restless _____
5. Usual life activities _____
6. Identification with the _____

The Grief Process

1. _____
2. Emotional _____
3. Depression and _____
4. _____
5. _____
6. _____
7. Hostility and _____
8. Inability to return to _____
9. _____
10. Struggle _____

How to Minister at a Time of Grief

1. Begin where the _____
2. Clarify his expressed _____
3. _____
4. Be sensitive to his feelings and don't _____
5. Don't use faulty _____ with him.

A Bereaved Person Needs

1. Safe _____
2. Safe _____
3. Safe _____

YOUR PERCENTAGE OF THE DECISION ANALYSIS

Describe the decision-making process of your marriage by indicating the percentage of influence you have, and the percentage your spouse has, for each issue. The total for each decision must be 100 percent. (Those who write 50:50 too many times will be considered dishonest.)

Decision	Percentage of My Vote	Percentage of Spouse's Vote	Who I feel is more qualified to contribute to this decision. (Write your initial for your spouse's.)
CHOICE OF:			
New car	_____	_____	_____
Home	_____	_____	_____
Furniture	_____	_____	_____
Your wardrobe	_____	_____	_____
Spouse's wardrobe	_____	_____	_____
Vacation spots	_____	_____	_____
Decor for the home	_____	_____	_____
Mutual friends	_____	_____	_____
Entertainment	_____	_____	_____
Church	_____	_____	_____
Child-rearing practices	_____	_____	_____
TV shows	_____	_____	_____
Home menu	_____	_____	_____
Number of children	_____	_____	_____
Where you live	_____	_____	_____
Husband's vocation	_____	_____	_____
Wife's vocation	_____	_____	_____
How money is spent	_____	_____	_____
How often to have sex	_____	_____	_____
Where to have sex	_____	_____	_____
Mealtimes	_____	_____	_____
Landscaping	_____	_____	_____
Various household tasks	_____	_____	_____

CONFLICT

Causes of Conflict

1.

2.

3.

4.

5.

6.

7.

8.

9.

10.

COPING WITH CONFLICT

Ways to cope with conflict are:

1.

2.

3.

4.

5.

6.

7.

8.

9.

10.

THE COUNSELOR'S GAME

Case 1

Most of my male friends would probably pay to have the problem I have until they had to live with it for three years.

Our sexual adjustment is very good, but my dear wife seems to have no idea that there are limits to a man's interest in sex. She seems firmly convinced of the myth that men are always eager, always capable and never tired, preoccupied, or just uninterested.

The few times I have tried to signal her to slow things down she seemed confused and hurt. Sex is great, but how do I introduce some moderation into the proceedings?

Case 2

We seem to have a great marriage. We both work, have a small apartment, and financially we're getting along well. After about six years of marriage, I stopped work when I discovered I was expecting our first child. We decided we'd have to have more room. The only way we could possibly buy a home of our own in the city was to get financial help from Dave's father. He was a widower and he was helping to provide funds for our new house; I invited him to live with us. I soon discovered that this was a mistake.

Dave was in partnership with his father and, little by little, their money blended into one fund. Dave gives me a small amount of money with which to pay bills and to buy groceries, but it does not stretch sufficiently to cover the costs. I have to ask not only Dave but his father, too, for money to run our home. And I have no money to purchase items for my personal needs. What should I do?

Case 3

We've been married eleven weeks, and Frank has just told me that with the fall coming on, he is planning four or five nights a month out with the boys, bowling or just doing some talking. He says we both need private lives and our own circle of friends and that I should make similar arrangements.

Now, I can buy occasional nights out, but this *planning* to be apart bothers me. I married him to be with him and to do things together. Besides, my girlfriends just do not go out much without their husbands. What do you suggest?

Case 4

If my mother-in-law makes one more comment on my cooking or housekeeping, I think I will scream. She has nothing at all to do, so she drops in two or three times a week and tells me what's wrong with my recipes, why I should change furniture polish, how the plant won't grow in that corner, and why I shouldn't spend money on having laundry done. There's never a word that comes out of her mouth that isn't some direct or implied criticism.

I keep telling Larry to shape her up on this matter. He says he knows his mother can sometimes be a pain but that I am too sensitive, too. Besides, he adds, I'm a big girl and can fight my own battles. What do you suggest?

(Cases 1 and 4 adapted from *Marriage: Discoveries and Encounters*. The Cana Conference of Chicago, pp. 11–12.)

CONFLICT ANALYSIS

Most persons have disagreements and conflicts in their relationships. Please indicate below the approximate extent of agreement or disagreement between you and your partner for each item on the following list.

	Always Agree	Almost Always Agree	Occasionally Disagree	Frequently Disagree	Almost Always Disagree	Always Disagree
1. Handling family finances	___	___	___	___	___	___
2. Matters of recreation	___	___	___	___	___	___
3. Religious matters	___	___	___	___	___	___
4. Demonstrations of affection	___	___	___	___	___	___
5. Friends	___	___	___	___	___	___
6. Sex relations	___	___	___	___	___	___
7. Conventionality (correct or proper behavior)	___	___	___	___	___	___
8. Philosophy of life	___	___	___	___	___	___
9. Ways of dealing with parents or in-laws	___	___	___	___	___	___
10. Aims, goals, and things believed important	___	___	___	___	___	___
11. Amount of time spent together	___	___	___	___	___	___
12. Making major decisions	___	___	___	___	___	___
13. Household tasks	___	___	___	___	___	___
14. Leisure time interests and activities	___	___	___	___	___	___
15. Career decisions	___	___	___	___	___	___
16. Praying and Bible study together	___	___	___	___	___	___
17. Child-rearing procedures	___	___	___	___	___	___

18. Where we live

19. The dots on the following line represent different degrees of satisfaction in how you presently resolve conflicts. The middle point, "satisfied," represents the degree of satisfaction of most relationships. Please circle the dot which best describes the degree of satisfaction, all things considered, of your conflict resolution level.

0	1	2	3	4	5	6
Extremely *Un*satisfied	Fairly Unsatisfied	A little Satisfied	Satisfied	Very Satisfied	Extremely Satisfied	Perfect

(Adapted from Graham Spanier, "Measuring Dyadic Adjustment: New Scales for Assessing the Quality of Marriage and Similar Dyads," *Journal of Marriage and the Family,* February 1976.)

FORGIVENESS
SENTENCE COMPLETION

1. Forgiveness is...

2. When I forgive another, I feel...

3. It is most difficult for me to forgive when...

4. It is easiest for me to forgive when...

5. When I have been forgiven by another, I feel...

6. In order for forgiveness to occur I must...

7. The first time I experienced God's forgiveness I felt...

8. The main question I have concerning forgiveness is...

9. Forgiving myself is...

10. The Bible teaches that forgiveness is...

AMERICAN FAMILY LIFE TODAY

BETTER HOMES & GARDENS—1972

71% said American family life is in trouble

64% said America is a worse place to rear children than 10–15 years ago

11% said most couples are well prepared for marriage

85% said religion has lost its influence on family life today

1978 REPORT

76% said American family life is in trouble

2500 FAMILY LIFE EDUCATORS AND COUNSELORS SAID:

66% of the churches are not doing an adequate job of promoting and maintaining family life

93% of the youth are not receiving adequate preparation for marriage from their parents

MARRIAGE ODDS

96% of Americans will marry

38% of these will divorce

79% of these will remarry

44% of these will divorce again